When Divorce is Right

J. BRUCE SOFIA, M.ED., D.D.

When Divorce is Right
ISBN: 978-0-9896518-3-7
eBook ISBN: 978-0-9896518-8-2
Copyright © 2014 by J. Bruce Sofia

Published by
Yorkshire Publishing
9731 East 54th St.
Tulsa, OK 74146

Text Design: Lisa Simpson
www.SimpsonProductions.net

Some Scriptures are taken from the New American Standard Bible®, Copyright © 1960, 1962, 1963, 1968, 1971, 1972, 1973, 1975, 1977, 1995 by The Lockman Foundation Used by permission. (www.Lockman.org)

Some Scriptures are taken from the New King James Version. Copyright © 1979, 1980, 1982 by Thomas Nelson, Inc. Used by permission. All rights reserved.

Some Scriptures are taken from the Holy Bible, New International Version®. (NIV®) Copyright © 1973, 1978, 1984 by International Bible Society. Used by permission of Zondervan Publishing House. All rights reserved.

Some Scriptures are taken from the Holy Bible, New Living Translation, copyright © 1996. Used by permission of Tyndale

All references to deity have been capitalized by the author and are not originally capitalized in some translations.

"Get out! Get out for your life's sake, for your children's sake, and for God's sake. *Mrs. A, Get out!*" I could not believe what I was hearing coming out of my own mouth. I confess, I had said those words in my mind before, but never out loud.

Divorce is a sensitive subject, which has affected over 50% of families in our culture today. Many questions surround divorce. Dr Sofia handles these questions with wisdom, tact, and biblical clarity. *When Divorce is Right* is a manual which gives us the "how-to-respond," and is a 'must have' for every library.

Huntley Brown
International Concert Pianist and
featured guest with the Billy Graham Association

When Divorce Is Right addresses divorce nicely from the Christianity (God) perspective. I will be using *WDIR* as a go-to-guide for my clients seeking divorce. We all have fallen short in our marriages in one way or another and *WDIR* gives us another chance to possibly get it right or to just move on in God's grace and mercy all together.

Dr. Bryana Carrea, DCC, BCLC
Founder & Executive Director,
Christian Counseling & Wellness Center for Women

With a database of over 25,000 clients and nearly 50% of them divorced, I heartily endorse this take on divorce as sheer brilliance. I love how *When Divorce Is Right* is empowering without being judgmental, and in chapter 11 there is hope with healing. Once again, Pastor Bruce, you have used the power of GOD to address modern day trials. I believe first hand this book is a gift.

Martino Cartier,
Celebrity Stylist and Motivational Speaker

From beginning to end, Bruce Sofia uses solid biblical doctrine to unveil the truths in God's word concerning divorce. Offering both encouragement and reproof, *When Divorce is Right* should be the handbook for those considering divorce, or better yet, considering marriage.

Dez Childs
Singer/Songwriter, Radio Show Host

The book *When Divorce is Right* is well written. Pastor Bruce Sofia concedes that God may look at divorce as a "broken mirror." There is a solution to a bad relationship in an honorable fashion. Pastor Sofia is correct in emphasizing the need to remove guilt on those who may have suffered through a divorce, which was justified. This is analogous to removing pain from an ill person, who suffers a malady, which he did not really contribute to with poor lifestyle, but he still feels guilty about having incurred.

Nicholas DePace, M.D., F. A. C. C.,
Author and Professor

Divorce can be one of the hardest things a person can go through. I know this first hand. In many ways it's like a death, and can nearly bankrupt a person spiritually. I believe that Pastor Bruce's writings can help many people facing this challenge, as well as those who might be in the process of remarrying. He exhibits keen insights into the spiritual aspects of these decisions. I've known Pastor Bruce for a long time and can attest to the fact that he's a man of God with a working knowledge of the Scriptures. If you are facing divorce or remarrying again, then I believe this book will guide you through them both in ways you'll never forget.

Michael English
Grammy Award Winner & Recording Artist

A challenging and thought-provoking exploration of biblical principles on what may be the most important issue impacting modern Western culture.

Robert Fountain,
Calvary Chapel Miami Beach &
Nat'l Police Suicide Foundation Trainer

Anyone who has had the privilege to sit under the anointed preaching of Dr. J. Bruce Sofia knows that he is a gifted preacher. His messages are scriptural, sane, spiritual, and relevant—the best of all combinations. Having had the privilege to take one of his books into my hands and begin to read, it is obvious that he is a gifted writer as well.

J. Gordon Henry
Former Executive Vice President for Academic Affairs,
Liberty University, VA

Tackling a delicate topic from a biblical standpoint, and holding to truths is a rare thing in a shifting society. When many choose to abandon sacred values in exchange for trendy and popular beliefs, it's more than rewarding to give honor to sound principles that are founded upon scriptural understanding. Accurately researched and written, this book will, no doubt, save the lives and marriages of many who read and adhere to the message. As so adeptly stated, "marriage is a picture of salvation." Great insight for those struggling with the issue, and also, excellent teaching for the next generation!

L. Wayne Hilliard
Musician, Songwriter, Conference speaker and Author

Pastor Bruce Sofia has never been shy about tackling the taboo/ tough questions regarding Christian beliefs. He once again delivers a concise and clear response to the question, "When is divorce right?" I'm positive that upon reading this book many will not only find clarity, but also healing without the fear of retribution.

Frankie Negron
Singer/Songwriter, Latin Singing Sensation

Bruce Sofia has done it again. He has given us an exhaustive treatment of a difficult subject, presenting it skillfully and biblically, but tempering it with pastoral love and sensitivity. This book will be a gift to those contemplating or going through divorce, dealing with its aftermath, or helping others that have known its unique pain. We can all benefit from *When Divorce is Right*.

Rob Schenck, D.Min.
Chairman, Evangelical Church Alliance
Lead Missionary, Faith and Action in the Nation's Capital

TABLE OF CONTENTS

CHAPTER ONE

✦

WHY *ANOTHER* BOOK ON DIVORCE?

For the first time in my pastoral life I said, "Get out! Get out for your life's sake, for your children's sake, and for God's sake. *Mrs. A, Get out!*" I could not believe what I was hearing coming out of my own mouth. I confess, I had said those words in my mind before, but never out loud.

She came to our Church through the youth group, and served in the church where Sheryl and I first entered full-time local Church ministry. In the work place she excelled at her job. He was strong, well-built and handsome — and professed to be a Christ follower. But he lived on the wild side of life and exhibited behaviors that raised all kinds of red flags. She, like far too many 'good' Christian girls, got pregnant. Wanting a marriage that would honor God, she set up counseling in accordance to my request and church policy. He never came with her — not one time; there was always an excuse. Reluctantly, I refused to do the wedding.

Miss A meant the world to Sheryl and me, but I just could not in good conscience say, "I'll officiate your wedding." Miss A went to the pastor of the church she was attending. He counseled against the wedding, as did I, but what was he to do — she was pregnant and they wanted to get married.

I can still hear her words — they ring loudly in my ears, "I knew it was wrong walking down the aisle."

The marriage was hell on earth, if there is such a thing. (Let's take a Holy Ghost detour, or maybe it's a JBS detour, but whatever it is, it's worth going there. I don't believe anything we go through in this life can compare to Hell. Seriously! There is a reason why Jesus died and it wasn't to provide *another* way, it was to give man a way out, a way to escape the eternal jaws of a place no one in their right frame of mind wants to go.) He beat her. While pregnant with child number three, he knocked her down a flight of stairs and then kicked her in the stomach, cursing and calling her every foul name not found in the dictionary. When he would become abusive, which was far too often, the two other children would scream out, "Mommy, Mommy!" Words that should be warmly delightful were, in this case, milk-curdling and terrifying.

The Hebrew word is *Selah*, essentially meaning, "Meditate on what was just said." What child could go unscathed having such memories indelibly etched into the deepest recesses of his or her mind?

Josh McDowell in his booklet *My Journey . . . from Skepticism to Faith*, which describes his childhood and how he came to know Christ, recounts that at the age of eleven he had pre-meditated his father's murder over and over again. He had seen his father beat his mother mercilessly too many times. "There was only one person I hated more than God," Josh recalls, "my dad."

As you can imagine, there's so much more to Mrs. A's story — infidelity, abandonment, and, lest I be remiss, "high-jacking the call." Could Mrs. A really fulfill her calling of a mother training her children "in the way they should go" in that environment? Yes, there are times — I wish I did not have to say it — *when divorce is right*.

Today, God has brought into the life of Mrs. A a wonder-ful, loving husband and father. The family still wrestles with the damage done to the children by her first husband, but God has been faithful and honored Mrs. A's pursuit of Him. She still attends the church she attended as a young teen when I was its Youth Director, serves faithfully sharing Christ, connecting people, and serving others. Yes, God majors in the impossible. He loves turning the uglies of life into something beautiful; and when we let Him, He finds the plus in a pile of minuses.

I must admit, it is with reluctance and great trepidation that I write, *When Divorce is Right*, not because I believe what I pen is wrong, but because in divorce everyone is a "victim." It is true, there are winners in divorce, Mrs. A was one of them, and so were her children. But everyone, to this day, is a victim.

I am convinced that there are two primary reasons why God hates divorce: One, everyone is a victim — even in the best of scenarios (Malachi 2:6), and two, divorce is a broken mirror of what God is — love (1 John 4:8).

However, the truth that God hates divorce, yet at times commands it, must be raised for God is truth (Exodus 20:2; John 14:6). What people do with the truth is between them and their Maker, but we cannot veer from the truth because someone may mishandle it. For example, we must continue to preach "salvation by grace" whether people cheapen grace by their behavior or not. Our obligation before God is to present the truth as we understand it. Why? Because the truth is: "We are saved by grace, through faith and not by works" (Ephesians 2:8–9). The same is true of divorce — there are times when divorce is right even though God hates divorce.

Let's expand on this truth a little further. We must, as the bumper sticker declares, "DO RIGHT and Give the Consequences to God." For example, we may 'hate' to give our kids a spanking, yet God clearly states, "the rod of correction drives folly out of the heart of a child" (Proverbs 22:15). Therefore, we, when merited, place the board of education on the seat of learning. Another example is that a person may hate taking a particular medication – they just don't like the way it makes them feel. However, because it cures the problem — they take it. Hence, even though God hates divorce doesn't mean He may not command it.

Why does God command divorce? So that the greater calling of accomplishing His purpose would be consummated (Ezra 10; 1 Corinthians 7:15). The ways of God are beyond us because we see in the temporal and God sees in the eternal (Psalms 145:3; Isaiah 55:8). God has not called us to death, other than dying to self for His glory and will — He has called us to life. It is true, at times we *win* by losing and we *live* by dying. Yet, in these instances losing *is* winning and dying *is* living. It's the "paradox of Christianity," as Charles Colson profoundly put it. Here's the key: no matter what God calls us to, it is life in abundance (John 10:10).

Wayne Monbleau, host of the popular radio program *Let's Talk About Jesus*, suggests that when Scripture is not black or white on a subject, the best barometer is to ask: "The decision I have to make — is it life or death?" If it is death, then most likely it is not of God for Jesus came to give life and that more abundantly (John 10:10). In some instances divorce is life — as in the case of Mrs. A. To remain in that marriage was death. God clearly calls us to an abundant life — in fact, that is the only life He gives – abundant and eternal.

Many argue that divorce is *never* right, and should a person divorce he/she can *never* remarry. If that were true then God would not have issued a bill (formal acknowledgment) of divorcement in the first place. The whole purpose for "a bill of divorce" was to formally validate (both scripturally and civilly) a couple's divorce and provide a means for a person to remarry (Deuteronomy 24:1–4; Isaiah 50:1; Jeremiah 3:8; Matthew 5:31).

Although in this book it is not my intent to exhaustively address the subjects of marriage, divorce, and remarriage, it is my aim to share insight and biblical substance to help the reader appreciate the heart of God in these matters. Experience has taught me that far too often those in the church get caught up in the legalities of Scripture and miss God's heart. It is with utmost humility then, that the purpose of this book is to lay hold of God's heart.

There is a reason why Jesus did not give instructions to the woman at the well who had five previous husbands and lived with a man to whom she was not married. Think about it! If Jesus had given instructions in this particular situation, far too many pastors, would-be-preachers, counselors, minister leaders, etc., would reference this as God's "how to" and apply it to almost every situation. In so doing, the advisor thereby would miss weighing the hearts of the individuals in each unique case. Is that not what our Lord does here? Accesses the woman's heart and *then* renders His decision and direction. Remember God sees what we cannot see — the heart (1 Samuel 16:7).

Jesus does not tell the woman at the well to go back to husband number one (that would transgress God's instruction in Deuteronomy 24:4), nor does He tell her to marry the man with whom she was living. What we do know is that she believes in Christ, her life is changed, and she becomes the first woman evangelist in the New Testament, seemingly converting her entire town to belief in Jesus as Messiah and Savior of the world (John 8).

Whatever it was this woman did with her marital situation, guaranteed, it was right — for she had come to know the One who never got it wrong. Ever! Recall her description of Jesus when she went back to her hometown, "He told me everything I ever did" (John 4:39b). Everything! Now, that's covering a lot of ground in a few minutes — or hours.

Although the scriptural narrative does not give us any further conversation between Jesus and this Samaritan woman, I suspect that she and He discussed her plight, and whatever it was that Jesus told her to do, she did it.

That is what God wants us to do, put each individual case on the altar of His Word and will, and seek His mind. Then, once we accept God's will, we must act in faith without doubt (Romans 14:23). The late Dr. Jack Hyles said, "There is no reason why the mind that was in Christ Jesus cannot be in us" (Philippians 2:5). Certainly, Dr. Hyles was correct. We are commanded to lay hold of the mind/attitude of Christ in all matters — including divorce and remarriage. Jesus said, "Ask, and it will be given to you; seek, and you will find; knock, and it will be opened to you" (Matthew 7:7).

If we ask, seek, and knock, then the mind of Christ will be given to us. Indeed our gracious, loving Heavenly Father will reveal the destiny He has designed for us, and grant us a peace that can only come from knowing we have laid hold of His will and are walking in it (Philippians 4:7; Colossians 3:15).

QUESTIONS

1) Have you ever told a person to get out of a marriage (to divorce)? If so, why?

2) What is the reason why the author gives us yet, "… another book on divorce?"

3) Why does the Bible not tell us what Jesus told the "Woman at the Well" regarding her "live-in" situation?

4) When Scripture is not black and white (absolutely specific) on a particular situation, what is a good barometer to use?

5) After reading this chapter, what question would you ask?

CHAPTER TWO

⊱⊰

APPROACHING THE SUBJECT

When I was in fifth grade there was only one student who came from a divorced home. I am sure there may have been others, but if there were no one knew it. Today, the scenario is altogether different.

A few years back my sister, Mrs. Sandy Clendenen, who teaches one of our third and fourth grade Sunday School classes, took prayer requests. On this particular Sunday, nineteen out of twenty-three kids wanted to pray that Mommy and Daddy would get back together.

That's the world in which you and I live!

I believe everyone, if not directly then indirectly, has been touched by divorce. Much is written about this subject today, but my observation is that few truly look at *all* God has to say. Furthermore, those who do look at the entire Bible typically self-select which passages they reference and then interpret the Scriptures in light of their own personal theological background, rather than objectively looking at all passages relevant to the subject. Certainly, I don't mean to be judgmental of those who bring their theological or philosophical backgrounds to this subject; if we are honest we'll admit this is true of all of us. For instance, the hymns we sing today for the most part are born out of human experience. Yet there was a time in the Church when only singing songs directly from Scripture was permitted. Both have their place and contribute to our worship experience (Ephesians 5:19). So our interpretation of subjects relational to our culture and society also emerge from human experience and they, too, have their place in the library of Christian thought. However, no matter from what posture we approach hymns, psalms and spiritual songs, or the subject of divorce – God's word remains our final authority.

Born out of the crucible of divorce, each chapter begins with a real-life scenario that sets the stage for the subject addressed. My purpose in writing this book is to lay hold of God's heart in every chapter, offering hope no matter how deep the pit. Corrie Ten Boom, a beautiful believer who endured the savagery of a Nazi concentration camp, put it this way: "There is no pit so deep that God's love is not deeper still."

God desires permanency in love and anything less shatters His ideal. As we explore His standard we will discuss the effects of not merely falling short of God's ideal, but shattering it as well. Because it is far too easy to bounce ideas around philosophically, apart from the tears that accompany a broken heart, we will address the *biblical license, allowance,* and *command* to divorce as scrupulously and forthrightly as possible. In so doing, I would like to explore the three biblical reasons divorce is permitted: abandonment, sexual infidelity, and hijacking the call, along with additional problems common to divorce.

For example, we'll look at the consequences of dating before one's divorce is final and the challenge of responding biblically to sexual infidelity. Why are sexual sins greater than all others? What is the difference between forgiving and forgetting? Is there a formula, *per se*, for restoration and "wiping slates clean?" These are real questions needing real answers that can bear up beneath the very real weight of reality in a complex world. Any answers, any solutions, other than God's heart as revealed in His infallible Word, fall painfully short of truly solving the problems facing those of us living in a Hollywood-ized, post-modern and post-Christian world. (Postchristianity [1] is the decline of Christianity in contemporary societies. It is the belief that the loss of the Christian monopoly in political affairs, especially in the Global North where Christianity had previously flourished, will eventually lead its demise in favour of secular nationalism.[2] It includes personal world views, ideologies, religious movements or societies that are no longer rooted in the language and assumptions of Christianity, at least explicitly, although they had previously been in an environment of ubiquitous Christianity, i.e. Christendom. Wikipedia)

While there is never a way around such challenging dynamics, only a way through them, it is important to consider the principles discussed for facing their aftermath in this book: What are some of the fundamentals for healing a broken heart? Who comes first, spouse or children? How do you make a blended family work? Are there realistic guidelines to entrusting the mess you've caused, or the mess you've found yourself in, to a sovereign God, believing that He will "work out all things for your good?" (Genesis 50:20; Romans 8:28)

It is my prayer that through our exploration of the subject of divorce, the Spirit of God will give us His heart. Let us become a generation that refuses to be ripped apart by divorce, while still giving those affected by divorce the measure of healing necessary to wipe slates clean, move forward in forgiveness (a two-way street, Matthew 6:14), and change the world in which we live by demonstrating God's love, God's way, to His glory.

QUESTIONS

1) What does the author mean when he says, "Few truly look at all God has to say" regarding divorce? Have you found that statement to be true or false?

2) Corrie Ten Boom says, "There is no pit so deep that God's love is not deeper still." Where have you found that to be true in your own life?

3) Although introduced but not discussed in this chapter, why are sexual sins greater than all others?

4) What is meant by "post-Christianity?"

5) After reading this chapter, what question would you ask?

CHAPTER THREE

⁓

I'M DIVORCED — WHERE DO I GO FROM HERE?

THEY MET IN CHURCH

They met in church, were young and in love. She was beautiful and turned heads wherever she went. He was handsome, the son of a pastor, and every girl's dream. It was a match made in heaven — so most everyone thought.

But the ending did not equal the promise. I remember. I went to court with the young man. The wife did not come to the courtroom or have representation. The judge awarded everything to the husband with the exception of one car, which was in the wife's name and that year's tax return from the Federal government — it was to be split. What happened?

I watched the marriage implode. It was tragic! When the apostle Paul explains that all other sins a person commits are outside of the body, but fornication is against his/her own body (1 Corinthians 6:13) — there are no limits to that truth. Her act, whether consensual or forced (the actual details of the story no one knows, except God) sent her life spiraling into a graveyard spin of drugs, alcohol, deception, and adultery. He, in the mean time, hid it from everyone. Yet keen observers knew something was not right because he had lost his joy for life and ministry — he was a walking corpse. If he remained in the marriage he would have lost his calling and possibly his own life. Yes, there is such a thing as the walking dead.

When a person or a couple comes to me for counsel regarding marriage, this is the advice I most often give, "Do everything in your power to keep your marriage together; there may be winners in divorce, but everyone is victimized in some way or another." However, in this case, I said, "Get out or your calling will be gone and so will your life! You're dying in front of everyone. You are no good to anyone… or God. You have all three biblical grounds for divorce: *abandonment, hijacking the call,* and *infidelity.* Before there are children, get out!"

Yet I must be honest, in my heart I prayed that the woman's lifestyle would change and the marriage could be reconciled. Sadly, nothing changed. And today, to my knowledge, still hasn't. Yes, there are times when divorce is right.

Today the young man, now approaching thirty, has remarried. It was absolutely amazing to watch how God placed the woman of His choosing into this man's life — so those close to him thought. But, that's still another chapter not written in this book.

HE WHO FINDS A WIFE

The Holy Scriptures tell us, "He who finds a wife finds what is good and receives favor from the LORD" (Proverbs 18:22). There is life after divorce. Where children are involved (there were none in this case), life becomes much more difficult and often complex, but God is greater than any circumstance in which one may find him/herself (Philippians 4:7). If we will let Him, and that really is the key — letting go and letting God — He will work out our messes for His glory (Genesis 50:20; Romans 8:28).

Someone has said, "God has a place in mind for you; simply walk with Him and He'll get you there," and indeed He will. While preaching through the Psalms, the Holy Spirit gave me this maxim: *God specializes in finding a plus in a pile of minuses.* When you're tossed about in a raging sea of minuses, are you able to lay hold of the plus — that's a lifeline? Whether you see it or not, the "plus" is there!

WITH HOPE IN MIND

With that *hope* in mind we will address "how" God finds a plus in a pile of minuses, navigates hope in a sea of despair, and if we'll let Him, makes us a better person because of our failures. In keeping with his own unbridled life style, the popular and controversial Oscar Wilde wrote, "Experience is the name everyone gives to their mistakes." And probably true at one time or another for everyone, other than Jesus Christ. The bold

French sculptor and genius Auguste Rodin said, "Nothing is a waste of time if you use the experience wisely."

So the prayer of this author is that all who read this book and have undergone a divorce, or two, or three — maybe even five like the woman at the well, will use their past wisely and be a better person for it: less judgmental, more loving and empathic. Recall, the author of Hebrews tells us we do not have a high priest who is unable to sympathize with our weaknesses (Hebrews 4:15). Amazing when we consider He knew no sin (2 Corinthians 5:21). But, that is our compassionate God.

Don't misunderstand the hope; there are consequences to sin and that is unequivocal. However, the psalmist said: "Before I was afflicted I went astray, but now I obey your word. You are good, and what you do is good; teach me your decrees" (Psalms 119:67–68).

I recall the words of the Grammy and Dove award winner, Michael English, after his "fall from grace" (he's been our guest at Gloucester County Community Church on more than one occasion). He said, "I may not be known by 'who's who' anymore, but I'm far more equipped to minister to others." How true! Sorrow and grief certainly are God's University. Speaking of the Christ, the prophet said, "He was a man of sorrows and acquainted with grief" (Isaiah 53:3). Add to that the words of Solomon, "For with much wisdom comes much sorrow; the more knowledge, the more grief," and we're seeing the picture — clearly.

Yes, God specializes in taking the ugliness of life and transforming it into something beautiful. In so doing, we become more like Him. However, that too is a choice — the difference is living in life or living in death.

QUESTIONS

1) What stands out most to you in the opening story of this chapter?

2) What is the connection between, "He who finds a wife finds what is good," and the Creation account?

3) What is meant by "God finds a plus in a pile of minuses?"

4) Can you cite a time where you found the above to be true in your own life?

5) After reading this chapter, what question would you ask?

CHAPTER FOUR

✑

MARRIAGE — THE ORIGIN AND ORDINATION

THE PERFECT MARRIAGE WITH ONE EXCEPTION

She would often say, "We have the perfect marriage." And I would think, "Except for one thing — you are unequally yoked" (Leviticus 19:19; 2 Corinthians 6:14). Now for those who are unfamiliar with the Bible and that terminology, let me explain for this is no trivial matter — it's huge and consequential. When a couple is "unequally yoked" there is a strong possibility that they have conflicting value systems, which will eventually collide.

In this instance the day came. The wreck took place. The value systems collided and the family was devastated. Mr. B (that's the name we'll give the husband) decided he wanted to live with another woman. You can imagine the ramifications. However, Mrs. B (that's the name we'll give to Mr. B's wife) began to place how she should respond on the altar of God's will. You might ask, "What does that mean?" It means she began to seek the mind of God. She wanted to hear from God; she wanted His advice, only.

No one had any problem with what she heard — at first, but after a year, two, three, four... yes even a decade, most weighed in with doubt, "Did Mrs. B *really* hear from God?" Furthermore, Mrs. B had "biblical" grounds for divorce — both abandonment and infidelity. Most thought, if not said, "Who would want him back anyway?" But, Mrs. B believed that God had told her to wait and watch because He was going to bring her husband back home. Honestly, if it were anyone else we all would have said, "Mrs. B didn't hear from God; she is hearing herself." However, Mrs. B has a love for God and a prayer life that is second to none; so we dared not question what it was she heard — at least not to her face.

Over the years Mr. B would come and go, returning to his girlfriend's house to retire for the evening. It ruined Mr. B's relationship with his sons. Fourteen years after the separation Mr. B started coming home more frequently and began moving his belongings back into the house. When Mrs. B would ask me how she should respond, I would simply say: "You can entertain but you don't have to be his 'whore.'" I never asked if there was any intimacy on those return visits, I figured that was between Mrs. B and God.

It was nearly fifteen years after Mr. B left to live with another woman before Mr. B moved back home with all of his belongings. Are things peachy with his sons? No. But, what Mrs. B believed she heard from the LORD has proven to be true, and I suspect God will, in His timing and His way, mend the relationship between Mr. B and his sons.

I'm reminded of Psalm 105:19 that says of Joseph, referencing the word of the LORD he received through dreams, "…till what he (Joseph) foretold came to pass, till the word of the LORD proved him true."

Has Mr. B given his life to Christ? Not yet. Will he? I don't know and Mrs. B hasn't said she heard from God concerning her husband's salvation. But she is believing and praying. And there's no better place to start than there.

FOUR TRUTHS FOUND IN MRS. B'S STORY

These four truths stand out in my mind concerning Mrs. B's story:

1. *We can lay hold of God's will.*

2. *When we hear what He has to say, we must be willing to wait until what He has promised comes to pass.* (For Abraham and Sarah it was twenty-five years; for Moses it was forty years.)

3. *If we are willing to wipe slates clean and trust God unconditionally, even fifteen years of infidelity cannot put asunder what God has joined together.*

4. *There is a certain peace that has no equal when you have heard God and obeyed.*

Now the reality is that the outcome may not always be that of Mrs. B's story. You may hear God say "wait" and have to be content with that. Furthermore, He may not tell you the outcome. Your husband/wife may not return, but at least you have the peace of mind and clear conscience that come from knowing you've obeyed God, done right, and entrusted the consequences to Him.

Recall, we are free moral agents and God seldom forces His will upon any of us. The Bible reveals that God interacts with man with respect to His desires for us in three ways: His *perfect* will (David shepherded Israel with tenderness and integrity), His *permissive* will (God allowed Israel to have a king, but that was not His first choice), and His *overriding* will (God would not allow Balaam to curse Israel at Balak's request).

CHANGE FOR THE BETTER

Isn't it fascinating how we find ourselves echoing the words of our parents: "Things have changed! When I was a kid … That's not the way we did it … Etc…" I must confess that I'm glad some things have changed. I have had my motorcycle license since I was eighteen. My first bike was a chopped Honda 450 with handle-bars that were too high to pass inspection. The bike would rattle my entire body a full hour after I climbed out of the saddle. I would dismount the bike with my hands and butt tingling as if I were physically impaired. Keeping with this subject of change, Harley's V-Rod will make it from one side of the United States to the other without seven repair stops along the way. Now it doesn't sound like the old Shovel Head, but it's far more reliable and a heck of a lot faster. (Try 112 mph in the quarter mile. That's fast!) I can hop a plane and be across the United States, Philadelphia to Los Angles, in five-and-a-half hours. And, I think we all like being able to send a letter clear across the world with the press of a computer key.

Think about it! We can see history being made as it happens; we can instantly have information in our hands that at one time would have taken days if not weeks, even months and, in some cases, years. I actually remember how people would discredit the Bible by saying, "How is every eye going to see Him?" — referencing the Scripture's description of Christ's second coming. The tragedy of 9/11 certainly dismissed that argument. We saw history in the making while it was happening — instantaneously!

Lest I be remiss and discredit the Almighty, be clear, God doesn't need TV for every eye to see Him; He is more than capable of making sure everyone sees Him with or without TV — but that's another subject altogether.

You would think that after 6,000 years of recorded history and 4,500 years with God's written Word in our hands, man would be honest enough to admit that God's Word will always prove itself to be our final authority for life, faith, and the practice thereof, as it does on the subject of marriage, divorce, and remarriage.

CHANGE FOR THE WORSE

However, there are things that have changed which are not for the better and they have impacted our society in a harmful way. Consider these alarming statistics:

- Over the last ten years the number of unmarried couples living together increased by 71% and only 10% of those "live-in" relationships will last more than five years. *Christian Law Association

- From 1999 to 2000 the number of single-father households increased by 62%; single-mother households increased by 25%. *Christian Law Association

- The current U.S. divorce rate is 41% as reported by the National Center for Health Statistics for the 12-month period ending in October 1999 (6 September 2000). *Americans for Divorce Reform

As of 2012, these were the latest statistics according to *Enrichment Journal* on the divorce rate in America:

- The divorce rate in America for first marriage is 41%

- The divorce rate in America for second marriage is 60%

- The divorce rate in America for third marriage is 73%

As I mentioned in chapter one, when I was in middle school there was only one person in my fifth grade class who came from a divorced home. (There may have been others but if there were, no one knew it.) Things don't always change for the better!

We could take time to identify the influences that have caused the breakdown of the traditional family and the tearing down of the marriage union, but that is not the purpose of this chapter. The purpose of this chapter is to lay hold of the mind and heart of God in this mysterious edict called "marriage."

THE ORIGIN/ORDINATION OF MARRIAGE

God ordained marriage in creation. In Genesis 2:18-24 we read,

"The Lord God said, 'It is not good for the man to be alone. I will make a helper suitable for him.'"

It is illogical to think that God would create us to live alone. If God wasn't alone in heaven, why would He predestine man to be alone on earth (Genesis 1:26)? We were created in *His* image — Father, Son, and Holy Spirit. Add to that a host of angelic beings: Seraphim, Cherubim, the twenty-four Elders, the four Living Creatures, a host of saints too numerous to count, and it is obvious that God is gregarious. He loves company. Not that He needs company, He doesn't — He is complete in Himself (Genesis 1:26; Exodus 3:14; Psalms 50:12; Psalms 135:6; James 1:17).

Man and creation therefore become a valued pleasure to God (Revelation 4:11), not a self-centered emotional need. Here is God's account of man's origin as stated in Genesis 2:21–23:

So the Lord God caused the man to fall into a deep sleep; and while he was sleeping, He took one of the man's ribs and closed up the place with flesh. Then the Lord God made a woman from the rib He had taken out of the man, and He brought her to the man. The man said, "This is now bone of my bones and flesh of my flesh; she shall be called 'woman,' for she was taken out of man."

Literally, the word for "woman" is "womb-man" or "man with a womb." In Genesis 5:1–2 God calls both the man and woman "man." Let's look at it:

This is the written account of Adam's line. When God created man, He made him in the likeness of God. He created them male and female and blessed them. And when they were created, He called them "man." [And in Genesis 2:24 we read], For this reason a man will leave his father and mother and be united (cleave) to his wife, and they will become one flesh."

ONE REASON WHY MARRIAGES FAIL

One reason why marriages fail is because the bride or groom does not leave his/her parents and become "one" with his/her spouse. I say this gently, but with unabashed assured-ness. God doesn't say that the man/woman is to be one (a soul mate) with his/her father or mother and or even with their children; we'll discuss this later when we address "the blended family." God commands that man and woman be one with his/her spouse.

This is why second and third marriages are less likely to succeed. With whom are you one? Your first wife? Second wife? Natural children? Stepchildren? Hopefully, this book will help you sort all of this out and find God's answers. Again, the call is to be one in flesh, that is, one spirit and one body with your *spouse*.

In Mark 10:2-9, Jesus reiterates this foundational principle concerning marriage. This is what we read:

> Some Pharisees came and tested Him by asking, "Is it lawful for a man to divorce his wife?" "What did Moses command you?" [Jesus] replied. They said, "Moses permitted a man to write a certificate of divorce and send her away." "It was because your hearts were hard that Moses wrote you this law," Jesus replied. "But at the beginning of creation God 'made them male and female.' 'For this reason a man will leave his father and mother and be united to his wife, and the two will become one flesh.' So they are no longer two, but one. Therefore what God has joined together, let man not separate."

I prefer the wording of the King James Version here: "For this reason a man will leave his father and mother and *cleave* to his wife." This old English word "cleave" implies "to be fastened to," like what happens when a person gets Crazy Glue on their fingers and they touch. To get them apart means flesh is torn away. Now that's being united or better worded, "cleaving" to one another and becoming one.

Jesus lifts up the IDEAL here: like God, ONE + ONE + ONE = ONE, not three. So it is with a husband and a wife: One + One = One, not two. (We will address what happens when the ideal is shattered in chapter 11, "Healing After Divorce.")

HOW IMPORTANT IS THE
INSTITUTION OF MARRIAGE TO GOD?

Consider this:

- The first institution ordained by God in creation was marriage.

- The first miracle performed by Christ was at a marriage.

- When Jesus returns for the church (those who have been blood bought and blood washed), Jesus is the *groom* and the church is the *bride*. The picture is one of a marriage. That's how important marriage is to

God. God not only calls a marriage to "oneness," He calls it to permanency.

GOD CALLS MARRIAGE TO PERMANENCY

As the nature of God is permanent, that is unchanging (1 Samuel 15:29, Hebrews 6:18), so it is the will of God for every marriage. Is that the reality? No, but it is His desire. Let's look at it in Romans 7:2–3:

> For example, by law a married woman is bound to her husband as long as he is alive, but if her husband dies, she is released from the law of marriage. So then, if she marries another man while her husband is still alive, she is called an adulteress. But if her husband dies, she is released from that law and is not an adulteress, even though she marries another man.

So if you want to be released from your spouse and not be an adulterer or an adulteress, a little arsenic may just do the trick. (Did a pastor just say that? Not me. I heard nothing.) The trouble with that advice is, guaranteed, you'll not get away with your crime. So, you have a choice: *live in a marital prison or a state prison.* The reality is that God did not intend marriage to be a prison but a place of safety, security, freedom, harmony, peace, and love.

Everything you can think of that is positive is what marriage should be. Does that mean there won't be difficult times? No! Hey, just the ordinary circumstances of life will seek to disrupt the permanency of marriage. But if you will invest in one another by dating and keeping God first, nothing will dissolve what God has joined together except death itself. I am reminded of the words of H. Jackson Brown, Jr., "Remember that a good marriage is like a campfire. Both grow cold if left unattended."

JUST FOR HUSBANDS

Now let me speak to just men for a moment — ladies you can skip this part. By dating I don't mean taking your wife to a ball game with another couple while you talk to the guy and she talks with his wife (or girlfriend). That's not a date! *A date is just you and her. Just you and her. Just you and her.* Like when you courted. Remember? Hey, you didn't want a third party around when you were courting. Three was a crowd! Remember? The two of you were all you needed. What happened? Oops, I won't go there, at least not for the moment.

JUST FOR WIVES

I know that we often live in a world of reverse roles compared to past centuries, that is, husbands stay at home and take care of the house and children while wives earn the larger pay in the work place outside of the home. However, I must confess, my observation is that men and women are designed with different constitutions; and I believe the Bible bears that out. Need we go past the basic biological functions of a man and a woman? I hope not. (Can you picture a man giving birth to or breast-feeding a child?) And, this is not the time or place to discuss these matters. As I addressed the men, so I would like to address you ladies. The Book of Wisdom says:

> Listen, my son, to your father's instruction and do not forsake your mother's teaching. My son, keep your father's commands and do not forsake your mother's teaching (Proverbs 1:8; Proverbs 6:20).

I grew up in *this* environment, and believe me — it worked. Not that Pop did not teach, at times he did, but Mom was much more suited for the profession. What I learned from my dad was more caught than taught. Now when it came to "instruction," Pop was — well, let's say, he had the heavier hand by far. He fulfilled his proverbial role.

I've been observing marriages, roles in the home and out of the home for over six decades and I believe, without question, that women are much better suited for caring for children than men, and men are much better suited for labor than women. Are there exceptions? Yes! Personality certainly plays a role in these things, but generally speaking I believe this holds true.

With that said, wives, you ought to create such an atmosphere at home that after a day at work your husband would rather come home to you rather than go anywhere else. Rather than having a beer after work with the guys (which may only get him in trouble), he should be saying: "My wife's waiting at home. Guys, I'm on my way home!" (If the role is reversed, then the wife should be saying, "Girls, my husband's waiting for me at home. Girls, I'm on my way home!")

Personally, a night out with my wife is better than watching the Devils whip the Flyers. Now I'm glad Sheryl understands my love of hockey and has no problem with me going to a game now and then. In fact, I don't think she has ever said, "No," but if it came down to hockey vs. Sheryl, I'd take my wife. (Well, I'd better be honest; I'd take her most of the time. If it's the Flyers vs Devils, or the Stanley Cup and tickets are available … I think you get the point.) Wives, make the home environment such a special place that your husbands want to come home before they go anywhere else.

MARRIAGE IS A PICTURE OF SALVATION

The Bible calls the revelation of Christ and the Church a "mystery" (Ephesians 5:32). Here's the picture! To be "saved" a person must:

"A" — **admit** that his/her sins have separated him/her from God (Psalm 14:1-3; Romans 3: 23);

"B" — He/she must **believe** that God did something about his/her sins in the person of Jesus Christ, the final Pascal Lamb/Messiah (Leviticus 17:10; Hebrews 9:19– 22);

"C" — **commit** him/herself to God's righteousness by confessing Jesus as Lord and Savior (Isaiah 53:5; Colossians 1:22);

"D" — **do** it today! (Isaiah 49:8; 2 Corinthians 6:2)

This is the very picture of marriage. The groom and bride both believe that **A** — they are incomplete without one another; **B** — that the person they are going to marry is their perfect match, that is, the right one for them; **C** — they then commit themselves to one another; and **D** — they have a day in which they do exactly that; it's called the wedding day.

JUST IN CASE

For those of you who have never received Jesus as your personal LORD and Savior for the forgiveness of sin, you can do that right now. Start with the ABCs and then pray the prayer given below:

"Father in Heaven, I'm sorry for the things I've done that are wrong: I am a sinner; forgive me. Thank You for loving me and sending your Son, Jesus, to pay the penalty for my sin. Holy Spirit, come into my heart; Jesus, be my Lord and Savior. I give You my life. Amen!"

Now that you've prayed to receive Christ, why not let me know? Go to *hijackedlife.com* and click on "The ABC's" then simply follow the steps given on the site or call **1-855-HJL-RSCU**. You can even respond the old-fashioned way: Postal Service and write: J. Bruce Sofia, 359 Chapel Heights Rd., Sewell, NJ 08080. (There's just something about getting a "hardcopy" of something in your mailbox — isn't there? Or am I dating myself?)

QUESTIONS

1) In the opening story of this chapter, what was the one exception to the "perfect marriage?"

2) What one phrase solidifies the ordination of marriage?

3) In what ways does the Creation Account refute same-sex marriage?

4) How is marriage a picture of salvation?

5) After reading this chapter, what question would you ask?

CHAPTER FIVE

DIVORCE — THE REASON *FOR* AND THE ALLOWANCE *OF*

IN LOVE AND ON FIRE FOR GOD, BUT THE FIRE WENT OUT

They began on fire for Christ and lived a life of wild abandon to His will. Ablaze with His love, no sacrifice was too great and no act of kindness too small. The kids came, and while they were among the poor of this world, life was a precious gift that they never took for granted and deeply appreciated. As one author put it, "When many couples had *less*, they had *everything* because they had each other." The lessons learned while being poor are rich beyond measure.

As time drifted on, forces from outside and inside eroded their relationship. Her deep-seated childhood wounds continued to bleed until the pressures of life drove her to embrace the darkness Christ had called her out of years earlier. She quietly became a closet alcoholic and grew increasingly numb, distant, and guilt ridden. The husband tried desperately to help and held things together for years, shielding their children from the facts, watching helplessly as the woman he treasured spiraled hopelessly out of control into a web of transgressions.

Keeping things together eventually became a hopeless endeavor; the cracks in his soul now became deep heartbreaking clefts. The kids were getting older and more perceptive. They began asking questions: "What's up with Mom?" Every day after work Mom would eat dinner, crash on the couch, or sit alone upstairs in the dark, for hours on end.

The storm of darkness tore through the family like a Midwestern tornado. The father realized that if he did not act drastically and soon, the venom that had poisoned his beloved would do the same to his children. It was death and not life. Didn't Jesus say He came to give life and that in abundance? It is the enemy, Satan, who comes to kill, steal and destroy (John 10:10). Furthermore, he kept hearing the words of Jesus when he said, "If anyone comes to me and does not hate his father and mother, his wife and children, his brothers and sisters — yes, even his own life, he cannot be my disciple" (Luke 14:26).

Don't be taken aback by our Lord's strong words here, specifically "hate." As in the case of Esau and Jacob, the 'hate' is, as Bible commentator Finis Dake says, "an idiom of preference." It is not a term expressing personal malice or jealousy in the sense we are familiar with, but a term contrasting God's attitude towards those who love spiritual things versus those who consider them of little value. Jacob valued spiritual things, things that had eternal value; Esau, on the other hand, despised them and lived for the moment. Jesus is saying (as I understand it), "Are you willing to love Me and that which counts for eternity, even at the cost of being rejected by family? Will you love Me more?"

Have you ever had to say to someone, "I love you, but I love God more." Painful words but absolutely necessary to our vocabulary as Christians.

Truly he loved his wife, truly he loved his children, but more than anything, he knew he had to love God supremely. God must be first. He would stand before God and give an accounting for his calling before and above all else. Jesus' words are clear; there is no ambiguity, there can be no misunderstanding — "Follow Me" (John 10:27).

How must he respond? This dysfunctional and sinful behavior was paralyzing him and affecting the children. Something had to be done and quickly. Reluctantly, he decided to get a legal separation hoping to shake his wife out of the self-absorbing and destructive behaviors she had embraced. If it worked he had gained everything, if it didn't, he was no worse off for it.

Sadly, her response only verified the reality, a reality that the children will never forget. Dad was left with no choice — for any semblance of life to remain in the home, for any hope of the children not being severely damaged, Dad had to pursue a divorce. Granted, in divorce everyone is a victim in some way or another, but sometimes losing is a far greater victory than winning.

The husband was awarded custody of the children and their property. With them came all of the legal expenses, which were massive. However, worse than the legal expenses he inherited was what he lost, something even more precious than his own life — his calling.

He had no illusions about his role, it always takes two, and mistakes were made on both sides for certain. The tragedy in this story is bigger than divorce; a strong passionate man of God was taken down, and the deep abiding love he and his spouse once shared for the Lord and each other was torn out by the roots and discarded like chaff.

Today he is alone, living a defensive, rather than offensive Christian life, plunged into the world of a single parent with all the struggles and hardships that come with it. A world he never wanted. But something tells me this will not be the end of the story. Proverbs 24:16 tells us, "…although a righteous man falls seven times, he rises again."

Now I may be wrong, but as I have come to know this man and observe his passion for the LORD, his desire to be a good dad and not degrade his former wife, everything that I'm seeing tells me this man's calling will be richer and more effective than he ever dreamed. Romans 11:29 says "…the gifts and calling of God are without repentance," and Genesis 50:20 tells us, "You intended to harm me, but God intended it for good to accomplish what is now being done, the saving of many lives." I find it absolutely amazing how God transforms the ugly into something beautiful when we let Him. And I suspect that's exactly what God is going to do in this instance.

OOPS, I MADE A MISTAKE!

This was not always a practice of mine, but I have made it such in the past few years of pre-marriage counseling. When I meet with a couple I ask this question of both the bride and groom to be: "Is there anything you would like to change about your future spouse?" If they say, "Yes," which in most cases they do, I ask what it is and if they can live with that annoyance if it never gets better (because most likely it won't — it may even get worse).

Sometimes it is much more than an annoyance, it is a character flaw. Character flaws are very serious issues because they will eventually fracture trust, and trust is the foundation upon which marriages are built. Correcting character flaws is a subject in itself, and must be discussed thoroughly before a couple says, "I do."

You can have a deep love for someone, but that doesn't mean you can live with him/her for the rest of your life. We've all heard the saying, "Love will find a way," and in truth it can. But — and that's a big "but" — it takes a great deal of humility on the part of both parties. Here's another spin on true love. Let's use John and Mary. If John truly loves Mary, and the two of them cannot get along, or he knows someone who is better suited for her, then he may rightly choose to not marry her because he wants what is best for her. True love wants what's best for the other person more than it wants for itself.

When a good friend and I transferred to the big University from Bible school, we decided to room together. After a semester of living with my friend, I said to him, "If we want to remain friends then we can't room together next semester." We parted company as roommates and have remained friends to this day. I was in his wedding and he was in mine. But rooming together just wasn't going to work. Two "cholerics" (the type A personality that by nature takes control) in the same room is like placing two bulls in the center of the ring when the cow's in heat — there's bound to be a collision.

When you have a roommate, more often than not, there is the understanding that the living situation will at some point change — that you can move out or move on. In a marriage, however, you don't have the option to say, "Oops! I made a mistake; I'm out of here!" Because, as we saw in the last chapter, you made a vow before God and have become one: One + One + One = One (You + Spouse + God = One). Furthermore, Ecclesiastes 5:4–7 tells us:

> "When you make a vow to God, do not delay in fulfilling it. He has no pleasure in fools; fulfill your vow. It is better not to vow than to make a vow and not fulfill it. Do not let your mouth lead you into sin. And do not protest to the [temple] messenger, 'My vow was a mistake.' Why should God be angry at what you say

and destroy the work of your hands? … Therefore stand in awe of God."

Children are the works of our hands. How many children's lives are altered for life because their parents made a vow and did not keep it? Far too many! Now, will there come a day when that child must answer for him/herself and stop shifting blame? Absolutely! A psychiatrist friend of mine, Dr Ira Fox, is in the midst of writing a book even as I type these words. His book is entitled *I Ate the Apple*. The theme of his book is this — a society that has learned to shift blame will never find a cure for what ails it. I recently read, "Are parents to blame when their children go bad? Potentially 'yes,' ultimately, 'no.'" How true!

Do you remember this scene in the Garden (Genesis 3)? After Adam and Eve sinned in the Garden of Eden, Adam blamed Eve and Eve blamed the serpent. And I suspect, although it is not written, that the snake blamed Satan and Satan blamed God.

THE "REAL WORLD" SHATTERS THE IDEAL

One + One + One = One. You + Spouse + God = One. That's God's heart. That's the ideal. That's God's perfect will. Anything other than that operates in the realm of God's permissive will. But the reality is that we live in an imperfect world, a world of shattered ideals, and marriage is one of them. What should our response be to this shattered ideal? First, we must offer healing, and second, we must raise a standard that mirrors God's perfect will, which is, "Till death do us part."

So, here's the outstanding question: *If it's God's will for a couple to be married until death separates them, why does God issue a bill of divorcement?* Let's look at the reasons why.

WHEN IS A SPOUSE GIVEN SCRIPTURAL GROUNDS TO DIVORCE?

Let's begin with the words of our Lord, "Some Pharisees came to [Jesus] to test him. They asked, 'Is it lawful for a man to divorce his wife for any and every reason?' Jesus replied, 'Moses permitted you to divorce your wives because your hearts were hard. But it was not this way from the beginning. I tell you that anyone who divorces his wife, except for marital unfaithfulness, and marries another woman commits adultery.' The disciples said to him, 'If this is the situation between a husband and wife, it is better not to marry.'" (Matthew 19:3–10).

The word used for "marital unfaithfulness" is *porneia, which means fornication or idolatry, not remaining faithful to being one; to unfasten what God has fastened; un-cleave the cleaving.*

It's important to note that Jesus does not give a new reason or license for divorce, it is the same reason laid down in the law. In Deuteronomy 22:13–14 we read:

"If a man takes a wife and, after lying with her, dislikes her and slanders her and gives her a bad name, saying,

'I married this woman, but when I approached her, I did not find proof of her virginity.'"

Jesus confirms what was written in the Law, the groom has grounds for annulment or divorce because the bride has come in dishonestly to the marriage bed. The same would be true for the man because God is no respecter of persons (Acts 10:34). The dishonesty spoken of here is relational to fornication (sexual immorality). Let's continue:

> "… then the girl's father and mother shall bring proof that she was a virgin to the town elders at the gate. The girl's father will say to the elders, 'I gave my daughter in marriage to this man, but he dislikes her. Now he has slandered her and said, 'I did not find your daughter to be a virgin.' But here is the proof of my daughter's virginity.'" Then her parents shall display the cloth before the elders of the town, and the elders shall take the man and punish him" (Deuteronomy 22:14–18).

So whether we are Old or New Testament, God clearly states a person *can* divorce for sexual infidelity. It is important to note that God doesn't say a person *must* divorce for purposes of infidelity, but they may.

There is one other passage of Scripture that addresses this matter indirectly. And although indirect, it is worthy of our attention because it reveals God's heart in this matter of divorce.

"This is how the birth of Jesus Christ came about: His mother Mary was pledged to be married to Joseph, but before they came together, she was found to be with child through the Holy Spirit. Because Joseph her husband was a righteous man and did not want to expose her to public disgrace, he had in mind to divorce her quietly" (Matthew 1:18-19).

MARY AND JOSEPH AND GOD'S HEART

Forgive me for getting personal here, but I love this passage because it reveals God's heart while at the same time telling us three things:

First, the reason why Joseph was permitted to divorce Mary, if her pregnancy was a result of promiscuity (and it wasn't), was because of sexual immorality.

Second, divorce is not always sin but what causes divorce is. Therefore to divorce a spouse with Scriptural grounds is not sin. The Bible says, "Joseph was a righteous man," and he was going to divorce Mary. God would not refer to Joseph as "righteous" if divorcing her was a sin.

Third, *how* Joseph was going to divorce Mary found favor with God. He wasn't out for blood; he wasn't looking to "get even," nor was he out to ruin her reputation or make himself look good. This was not about Joseph's image. No, Joseph truly loved Mary. The Bible says that, love, "...keeps no record of wrongs" and "...always protects" (1 Corinthians 13:5 and 7 respectively, known as the *Love Chapter*). In more cases than not, the way in which a divorce is handled, even by those who profess to believe, dishonors God.

Two things in reference to divorce become clearer to me the more I study and seek God's heart on this subject:

1) When a person divorces *for* another, that is, puts away a spouse with the intention of marrying another person, this transgression is extremely grievous to God. This is why Jesus says, "…if a person marries an adulterer that person is an adulterer." And what if the person who marries the adulterer was not guilty of adultery? What is the reason for this statement by our Lord? Motive! God is focusing on the motive. God is always looking at the heart — the reason *why* we do what we do. Others may see the end result of what we do, but God is more concerned with "why" we do what we do.

2) The biblical license to divorce is linked more closely to our "calling" than anything else. (We'll examine this statement in a moment, and more thoroughly, in chapter 7: "The Command to Divorce.")

MARRYING *FOR* ANOTHER

When you read Jesus' words in Mark 10:10-12, one word drives the content —"another.""Another" focuses on the motive for the divorce. Let me illustrate: We had this very situation occur in our Church. A man and a woman, both with positions of high visibility had very unhappy marriages. Eventually they both filed for divorce — on the same day.

The Advisory Board and I walked with both of them through their divorces concurring that they, respectively, had biblical grounds for divorce. To say that this experience was painful is an understatement. We had come to love their spouses as much as we did them. In fact, all four of them (husbands and wives) were employed by the church in some capacity at one time or another.

The couples worked together, vacationed together, and served together. So when the man and woman who were in positions of high visibility filed for divorce, we made it clear that they could not become an "item." (There were strong indications prior to and during the divorce process that made us believe they might have an interest in one another.) With that in mind, these persons would then be divorcing 'for' another. Therefore, our position was that before God they would have to answer for their divorces (as does anyone who goes through a divorce), but before the LORD and the congregation we must answer to God. Hence, any appearance of "spouse swapping" was something we could not put our approval upon. Remember why John the Baptist lost his head? He told Herod it was not right for him to have his brother Phillip's wife. (Herod had divorced 'for' another. To us the scenario was the same and it was wrong for either of them to have one another. And I believe we had the mind of God on this matter.)

One month after their divorces went through they secretly married. But a secret of this magnitude doesn't stay secret for long; one month later we found out that they were married. It was such a crushing blow to all of us who had loved them and given them support hoping for the best. There are times when motives are exposed and I believe this was such a case; they had divorced 'for another.' (Before God I hope I'm wrong, but I don't believe I am.) Even more tragic is that they disqualified themselves from their calling. They forfeited the very thing for which each of us will give an account — our calling.

Now, the question arises: Can't God forgive and restore those who are His (with His calling upon their lives), after we have disqualified ourselves? Absolutely! However, the prerequisite is repentance. When genuine repentance is demonstrated, God then chooses, in His way and timing, to use those who have blown it. (I would venture to say, most of us in one way or another have failed to repent immediately when we are doing or have done something wrong.) With that said, if we have disobeyed God in the nature of our divorce, God cannot use us until genuine repentance has taken place. God will put our calling, and us, on hold until we make right our wrongs. (We will deal more with this subject matter specifically in Chapter 14.)

Now, here's the beauty of our God, it is what makes Him different than us, what sets Him apart from all others – if we pursue Him in humility He *will not* discard us. Psalm 103:2-4 tells us,

"Bless the LORD, O my soul, And forget none of His benefits; Who pardons all your iniquities, Who heals all your diseases; Who redeems your life from the pit, Who crowns you with lovingkindness and compassion; ..."

I am grateful for His lovingkindness as I am sure is this couple, today. *Lord, give us Your heart of compassion and lovingkindness so that the world will know we are Christians by our love for one another. May the value and purpose for which we were created, the promise and potential with which You stamped us unfold in accordance to Your eternal plan. Forgive our transgressions and give us the strength to not go back to our sin. Let our lives be purged from all that hinders us from being used by You for Your will, Your way and Your glory. Remember that we are but clay in need of You every moment of every day. Grant us Your compassion and mercies daily. Hear our hearts when we say, "We love You."*

IN SUMMARY

Some would argue that once a person divorces, if they remarry they have committed adultery. And certainly in some cases that is true. *The Message* puts it this way:

> "Too many of you are using [divorce papers] as a cover for selfishness and whim, pretending to be righteous just because you are 'legal.' Please, no more pretending. If you divorce your wife, you're responsible for making her an adulteress (unless she has already made herself that by sexual promiscuity). And if you marry such a divorced adulteress, you're automatically an adulterer yourself. You can't use legal cover to mask a moral failure" (Matthew 5:32 /TM).

With that said, Jesus doesn't say a person cannot marry after divorce. If that were so then Jesus would not have put credence upon a "bill of divorcement" (Old or New Covenant). Furthermore, if the intent of Jesus' words was to deny a person the right of remarriage after divorce, He would not have addressed a "Bill of Divorcement," only the sin of remarriage. The Holy Scriptures clearly give reasons and allowances for divorce with the license to remarriage after divorce.

Keep in mind that a biblical and/or state divorce doesn't mandate remarriage. Paul cautions the Corinthian church that in Christ all things may be permissible, but certainly not all things are beneficial (1 Corinthians 6:12). In many cases remarriage is not only a poor decision, it's a bad decision, for which the children and family pay a very heavy price.

What happens if the person who remarries is the adulterer? Does that place him/her in perpetual sin? If the answer is yes, then there is little hope for any person born of human seed, for we too have committed sins for which we will pay the consequences (on earth) for the rest of our lives. One cannot sow and not reap, it's an irreversible principle. However, pertaining to eternity, God does not hold the believers' sins against them. That is why we (the believers) are referred to as "saints" (Ephesians 1:2; Philippians 1:2). Hebrews 10:11–14 is clear:

> "But when this priest (Jesus) had offered for all time one sacrifice for sins, He sat down at the right hand of God. ... because by one sacrifice He has made perfect forever those who are being made holy."

What does God expect of every believer? What should be etched upon our hearts? It is this: when we do sin, because we desire to please Him, we confess our sins and He who is faithful and just forgives us our sins (1 John 1:9). In this way we walk "in the light" and not in darkness (Isaiah 2:5; Ephesians 5:8; 1 John 1:7).

QUESTIONS

1) In the opening story of this chapter, what killed love?

2) Have you ever made a mistake in love? If so, what would you do over if you had to do it again?

3) Why do the Holy Scriptures regard Joseph as a "righteous man?" Give an example of a person you know who went through a divorce and acted "righteously" when the situation gave him/her cause to do otherwise?

4) What is meant by "marrying *for* another?"

5) After reading this chapter, what question would you ask?

CHAPTER SIX

≈

WHEN GOD WRITES A SUMMARY OF YOUR LIFE — HE DOES IT WITH RESPECT TO YOUR CALLING

Reverend P pastored a megachurch before there was such a thing as a megachurch. People came from three different states to two different campuses. In fact, before it was in vogue, he had a Saturday night service and hundreds attended. His small groups flourished; they were the heartbeat of the church. They were so tightly run that one may have considered them "cultish." It was amazing what he accomplished. Then it all fell apart.

Sadly, sin crept in. Some of the small group leaders would go away and swap spouses for a weekend. It was rumored that Pastor P, "the big chief," was having an affair. No one is sure what was true, only that eventually he divorced his wife and married another, the one with whom he was reported to be having an affair.

Some of the small group leaders did their best to hold the work together, but it failed. Eventually, the power struggle and false prophesies (personal and church related), destroyed the remnant. To this day, when Pastor P's name is mentioned there is a sense of awe ... and disappointment. Awe in that thousands of lives were changed by this man's ministry, disappointment in that, for many, "the end" is what is remembered. Many of those changed by Pastor P's ministry tried to resurrect what "they had," but it was not to be.

As a pastor, I have observed the parishioners who came to Gloucester County Community Church, from this man's churches; some came in our very first year. They have remained solid, steady and contributing parishioners. They are not takers. They live and demonstrate the fundamentals of our Christian faith by sharing Christ, connecting with people and serving others. They pray, tithe, serve, give alms and attend Church faithfully. They are the dream of every pastor.

Something is to be said for this man's labor in the vineyard. These people are the fruit of Pastor P's labor. His crown, as the Apostle Paul put it (Philippians 4:1). I'm not sure how people see P today. I have met him once. I am saddened by what took place in his life, and even more saddened by what happened to the work God had entrusted to him. I'm not sure how God would summarize P's life. I know how others do. However, the only summary that counts is God's. So I'll not pass judgment; I will, however, give thanks eternally for the good people Pastor P scattered among us to which we, as pastors, have all become beneficiaries.

If I had to write a summary it would read something like this: "Pastor P, I'm sorry I never had the opportunity to know you. I wish that I had. Please know that I'm deeply sorrowful for what happened to you and the work God entrusted to you many years ago. I am forever indebted to you for the wonderful parishioners that you shaped early in your years who today continue to serve the LORD faithfully, to whom so many of us have become the beneficiaries. May our gracious LORD reward you on 'that day' for your contribution to the Kingdom with these words, 'Well done good and faithful servant, enter into the joy of your Master' (Matthew 25:21)."

GOD'S SUMMARY OF A PERSON'S LIFE IS ALWAYS IN LIGHT OF HIS/HER CALLING

Think this through! When God summarizes the lives of men and women throughout the Holy Scriptures He ALWAYS does so in light of their calling. If there is an exception please tell me. A person doesn't answer for their friends and family; he/she answers for "obeying the call." (Although certainly the New Testament makes it clear that an "overseer" must be able to govern his household.) Let's look at a few examples of men and women answering to their call above all else:

- Adam and Eve were to tend The Garden, take care of the earth and not eat from the tree in the center of the garden (Genesis 1:26-31);

- Noah was to build an ark and preach repentance (Genesis 6-7);

- Moses was to lead Israel out of captivity, which he did at the cost of leaving the pleasures of Egypt (Hebrews 11:24-28);

- King David was to shepherd Israel, which he did with integrity of heart and tender care (Psalm 78:72);

- Mary was to be the mother of the Christ child (Luke 1:26-38);

- The Apostles were to take the GOSPEL to "all the world and make disciples," which they did at the cost of their own lives (Matthew 28:19-20).

Ultimately you and I will stand before God and give an account for whether or not we did what God asked us to do. He will take NO excuses. He tells the crowds in Luke 14:27 that they must "hate" (yes, that's a strong word) everything, even their own family (parents, children, and spouse) if they get in the way of "following Him." He must be first. He must be LORD of our lives. That's why God calls us to deny ourselves and follow Him. As Moses denied himself the pleasures of Egypt to enjoy the eternal pleasure of hearing God say, "Well done," so must we.

THE CALLING IS "BEING"
WHICH TRANSLATES INTO "DOING"

Please understand that when I use the word "calling" I am speaking of *being* who God has called us to be. Therefore as we "become more like Him" and submit to His will for our lives, our submission will ultimately translate into becoming a surrendered servant who seeks to *do* His will; that's the calling.

Forgive the Holy Ghost detour. How many times do I hear, "I don't know what God wants me to do with my life?" I'll respond, "It's not complex. We all have the same calling — just different pulpits. The calling is to 'follow Him and fish for men' (Mark 1:17). EVERY believer has the same calling, which is to follow Christ and win the lost to Christ. Now where we do that is our pulpit, and that certainly has many faces. But again, all the same aim. The same calling. The same purpose."

In writing this book (and a series of others), I have become friends, in a rather unique way, with Edward R. Kern, affectionately known to most of us as "Rick." Rick is an accomplished writer in his own right, and has ghostwritten for many well-known personalities and organizations. I met Rick at a "Faith and Action" roundtable gathering in Washington, DC. (Faith and Action is a missionary outreach to Capitol Hill directed by the Reverend Dr. Rob Schenck.) While conversing, I mentioned that the LORD had placed in my heart the command to write a book addressing "when divorce is right."

As you can imagine, we became engrossed in a deep and lengthy conversation about divorce. That was the commencement of our relationship. Because of his interest in the subject, particularly in light of the church, he agreed to allow me to bounce my material off of him. Need I say anymore? It is not only this topic that we are addressing from God's perspective, but the *Hijacked Life — Rescue Your Dream* has become a series of books addressing suicide, homosexuality, fornication, self-worth, cremation, Where did evil come from?, fortune telling, love, and many others subjects where Satan has caused the world and the Church to believe the lie. Let's not forget that every transgression/sin is rooted in the lie. It began in The Garden when Satan said to Eve, "Did God really say?" (Genesis 3:1). And that's what Satan continues to do today — ask the question, "Did God really say…" Fornication is wrong? Homosexuality is off limits? And the list goes on. Same old devil. Same old tricks. Same old tactics. Nothing new about the Serpent.

Rick has such a heart for God and the things of God; furthermore, he's extremely good at what he does. I could not have asked for a better writing companion in these projects. It is truly amazing what God can do when two ask in agreement and touch any one thing (Matthew 18:19).

Back to the calling *to be*: It really does begin with the enemy convincing man to believe "the lie." And once he/she does, their calling is hijacked. All that promise and potential gets derailed. Think on this! Everything Satan offers appeals to our ego/flesh. For example, he tells us to have sex *before* we're married. After all, how do we know if you're compatible in that area? Isn't that what marriage is all about — sex?

What's the result of a relationship driven by sex? The lust that drives the relationship lies, it deceives participants. It hides the fact that emotional needs are *not* being met, other than the twenty minutes of copulatory bonding. Because lust drives the relationship, the flaws in the relationship are hidden until they're a few years into the marriage. At this point someone, if not both persons realize, "I really don't like this person. We really don't get along. We don't see eye to eye on anything." (We discuss this thoroughly in the Hijacked Life book, *Fornication — the Lie that Drives our Times.*)

After Rick read the section in this book on "the call" we had a rather interesting conversation. I said, "Rick, this is going to be extremely controversial. Many people are going to write this off as heretical." "But, it isn't," Rick said, "Nothing could be more on the mark." Rick went on:

"Listen, people will be up in arms about *When Divorce is Right* (WDIR), feeling as if marriage antedates and trumps 'the call'. It might be wise to give some serious thought about taking this one by the horns and differentiate between 'God's call *to do*' and 'God's call *to be*'. People make vocational sacrifices for the betterment of marriage all the time, working less hours or declining a promotion because it would take too much from their home life (qualitatively as well as quantitatively). But 'the call to be' is far different, and though it bleeds into 'the call to do,' the consequences of messing with it impacts everything we are, do, and touch. I am saying this just to provoke a bit of thought and throw my two cents in because I am certain this will arise as a public matter, even among your flock."

Rick continued, "In my book you are certainly right, marriage must support the call. Yet I think not just in action and intent, but by nature: it is part of the fabric of the two being one flesh. So, I will be praying! It is a big deal — and you will take it on one way or another." And, that is what I do in this book, take on the question: *Which is greater — the calling or marriage?*

And Mr. Kern, who is also a reverend, is right. One cannot separate the call *to be* from the call *to do*. Jesus' call *to be* was fulfilled in His call *to do* which took Him to the Cross. It's in being who God wants us to be that we fulfill the calling. And nothing in God's book supersedes this truth. That is why in Ezra, God commanded the priests to divorce their heathen wives.

THE EXCHANGE IS NEVER WORTH IT

How sad to watch a man or woman exchange his or her "calling" for a moment of transitory pleasure. Please believe me when I say I'm not being judgmental. I suspect we've all been there one time or another — where the only thing that matters is "my" immediate satisfaction and "my" right to be happy. But it's NEVER worth it. Consider this! Throughout the Psalms when the writer wanted you to consider what was just said, he would say, "Selah." (It means "to ponder or meditate upon.") Consider Esau, he sold his birthright for a bowl of soup. Reuben lost the rights of the firstborn for a roll in the hay with his father's wife/concubine. I cannot speak for all, but I know that I've done some pretty stupid things that could have cost me my birthright, but for whatever the reason, God was merciful. Funny! Well, not really! But think of the times when, "… be sure your sin will find you out," (Numbers 32:23) and it did. And you said to yourself, "Thank you Jesus it was not someone else who found me out." Now that's mercy, if not grace. Well, time to get back on the main highway!

If it breaks our hearts to watch people forfeit their calling, how much more does it crush the God who placed that calling in their hearts, and loves them with a never failing love. Recall when God removed the kingdom from Saul, son of Kish, and gave it to David, son of Jesse? God said through the prophet Samuel that it was His desire for Saul and his children to be over the Kingdom of Israel for all time (1 Samuel 13:13), but because of his disobedience God gave it to *a man after His own heart*. I truly believe God's heart was broken at this point; that He was crushed at the disqualification of King Saul. And I believe His heart is equally crushed when His children must be removed from their calling because of their selfish transgressions.

If indeed the calling of God is without repentance (Romans 11:29) then those giftings never leave us. However, where we use them is directly relational to our integrity and purity of heart. (We'll look at this more deeply in just a moment.)

Recently I met with a man whom the LORD put into my life some years ago. I was an instrument (there were others) that God used to take him off of the street, save his marriage, and place him in ministry. Now off the street and living for the LORD, he was facing still another hurdle — throwing all that God had rescued away for "a moment of pleasure," which was guaranteed to end like the Titanic. I pleaded with him to make the right choice, to not lose everything that was truly valuable to him — his marriage, his church, and most of all, his calling. The last I heard, he had bought the lie. He lost it all. My heart weeps! God's heart weeps more.

There is, however, a hope upon which I cling and that's found in Romans 11:29. God tells us that His calling is "without repentance." It is my prayer that the couple mentioned at the beginning of Chapter 4 would admit their sin and ask forgiveness — first of God, then of those whom they have offended. In so doing they will open themselves up to be used of the LORD to accomplish His purposes in *full* measure. I pray the same for the man just mentioned who has left his calling to pursue fool's gold. How did Shakespeare put it in *The Merchant of Venice*? "All that glitters is not gold."

A PLUS IN A PILE OF MINUSES

Now the reality is, when we blow it we may never fulfill our calling on the same scale as before, or in the same capacity, but God specializes in finding a plus in a pile of minuses *if* we will let Him. I love how God turns the "uglies of life" into something "beautiful." It's who He is! It is what He specializes in. It's what He did at Calvary, turned the ugliest moment in history into something beautiful. As the songwriter put it:

When God Writes a Summary of Your Life —
He Does it with Respect to Your Calling

"At the wonderful, tragic, mysterious tree

On that beautiful, scandalous night you and me

Were atoned by His blood and forever washed white

On that beautiful, scandalous night."

What a miraculous, omnipotent, awesome God we serve!

QUESTIONS

1) The opening story in this chapter sets the tone for writing a summary of a person's life. Would you write the summary of Reverend P's life differently than the author?

2) What is meant by "God's summary of a person's life is always in light of his/her calling?"

3) What is God's calling upon your life?

4) What would you write as a one-sentence summary of your life in relationship to your "calling?" Do you know what your calling is?

5) After reading this chapter, what question would you ask?

CHAPTER SEVEN

✑

DATING WHILE SEPARATED OR IN THE MIDST OF A DIVORCE

HE HAD A GIRLFRIEND, HIS WIFE WAITED, HE WISHED HE HAD, TOO

His story was intriguing. He was an atheist and came to a Sunday night concert with a group of male friends with the sole purpose of making a mockery of the service. But God had other plans. At the close of the concert when the invitation to receive Christ was given, he surprised everyone by publically coming forward and giving his life to Christ.

I remember that moment quite distinctly because it was the first time I had ever given the Invitation in a service. Up to that point the Invitation had always been given by our senior pastor. At the time I was serving as Director of Youth under Dr. Eugene Huber at the United Methodist Church in Pleasantville, NJ. Dr. Huber would bring in music groups every Sunday night for the sole purpose of evangelism.

The now-former atheist was married and had young children. Eventually his wife's curiosity got the best of her: what changed her unbelieving, "hell-raising" atheistic husband to a believing church goer? It wasn't too long after that when she started attending church and gave her life to Christ. Desiring to grow in Christ, Mr. M and his wife joined our Young Married Fellowship.

At the time a referendum (which I voted against) was on the ballot to permit gaming in Atlantic City. The ballot passed and this young father became one of many who changed professions as the gambling industry created numerous job openings. He was also one of many who found himself drowning in the industry's sea of wicked enticement. Soon the influence of the gaming trade wreaked havoc on his personal walk with the LORD — and marriage. Sadly he met a girl considerably younger who solicited his attention, emotionally, spiritually and physically.

This young father filed for divorce against the warnings of his pastors, those who loved him, and, more importantly, God's Word, which states, do not divorce *for* another. (See Chapter 4, section: "Mary and Joseph and God's Heart.") His wife waited, prayed, and refused to date, giving her children — all three of them, the attention they needed. She would wait on the LORD and trust Him to meet her needs until the horizon was biblically clear.

He remarried.

Got divorced.

Remarried again.

God honored the wife's commitment to wait on the LORD. Choosing to remain in the home and marriage, she did not retaliate in anger, bitterness, or envy during their separation. She didn't explore the field of available men — even after the divorce; and she easily could have. Attractive, pleasant, and fun to be around she was any man's catch (if you didn't mind little fishes coming with the catch). God honored her commitment to rest in her singleness. Sometime after her husband had remarried, divorced and remarried, God brought a wonderful man into her life whom she married and today serves with in full-time ministry.

I have spoken with her first husband on occasion. He says, "The worst thing I ever did was divorce "C" (his first wife). There is a time and season for everything under the sun. Dating while separated or in the midst of a divorce is not one of them (Ecclesiastes 3:1).

THE GENESIS OF THE SUBJECT

It was September 1996 at the conclusion of an 11:00 a.m. Sunday service that I mentioned in passing the subject of dating while in the midst of separation or divorce. The sermon focused on "The Heart of Rebuke." A couple leaving the church that afternoon thanked me for addressing the subject because it was where they were in their relationship.

That week I received phone calls, letters (e-mail was relatively new, in fact, I was still writing my sermons out longhand), and numerous requests for counseling appointments. All were directly related to my few comments said at the close of the sermon regarding "dating while in the midst of divorce or while separated." Obviously what was said touched a very sensitive nerve.

THE *LIE* IN DATING DURING SEPARATION OR IN THE MIDST OF A DIVORCE

First of all, we must let God be God. No one knows how a separation or a divorce will end. We may suppose, we may presume, and we may assume, but no one knows the final outcome but God.

Let us never forget that God specializes in the impossible. The angel told Mary the mother of our Lord, when referencing Elizabeth's pregnancy (Elizabeth was the mother of John the Baptist), "Nothing is impossible with God" (Luke 1:37).

THE DEVIL'S ADVOCATE

When couples separate, the husband or wife must guard against the lie of the enemy that says, "You deserve more than this." This is the lie of Satan. It is his tactic and it's nothing new — Satan will *always* appeal to your pride in some way or other. This truth is painted so well in the movie adaptation of Taylor Jackford's suspense melodrama *The Devil's Advocate*.

In brief, Kevin Lomax (Keanu Reeves) is a successful defense attorney in Gainesville, Florida; he has never lost a case. As the movie opens, Lomax is defending a schoolteacher, Mr. Gettys (Chris Bauer), against a charge of child molestation. As the trial progresses, Kevin comes to believe his client is guilty. During a recess, a reporter speaks to Kevin, saying that, "Nobody wins 'em all." Kevin still decides to go forward and wins the case after a harsh cross-examination of the young witness (Heather Matarazzo) by destroying her credibility.

At a celebration after the conclusion of the trial, Kevin is approached by a representative of the New York law firm of Milton, Chadwick, & Waters, who offers him a large sum of money to help the firm with jury selection. After his selected jury results in a not guilty verdict, John Milton (Al Pacino) invites him to join the firm, offering a large salary and a swanky apartment. Kevin accepts and moves with his wife Mary Ann (Charlize Theron) to Manhattan despite warnings from his devoutly religious mother (Judith Ivey) about the sinfulness of big city life.

It doesn't take long before the greed, corruption and "vanity" destroy everything that Kevin holds dear and John Milton (Al Pacino) is revealed for who he is — Satan. The twists and turns in this story are frighteningly true to life — the Devil is a liar; he comes to kill, steal, and destroy (John 8:44, John 10:10).

In a bizarre turn of events Kevin is transported back in time to the recess of the Gettys trial, and given the opportunity to reverse that moment when he won at any cost. Upon returning to the trial, Kevin, this time, announces that he can no longer represent his client, despite the possibility of being disbarred. A reporter, the same one from the first scene, follows Kevin and Mary Ann, offering to interview Kevin about his decision, saying he will be a star. After some prodding from Mary Ann, Kevin accepts the offer [to be interviewed]. After Kevin and Mary Ann exit the courthouse, the reporter shape-shifts into Milton and says with a sly grin: 'Vanity — definitely my favorite sin'. *quotations taken from <u>Wikipedia, the free encyclopedia</u>

In other words, Satan will appeal to our pride whether the cause is just or unjust, righteous or unrighteous. This is why God doesn't judge as man judges, but looks at the heart (1 Samuel 16:7; Isaiah 11:3).

It is what Satan, the serpent, did in the Garden. He appealed to the pride of Eve and Adam. He offered them more than what God had promised. Tragically they bought it. And look at where it got them… and us. Couples or individuals who are in the throes of a divorce or separation must be particularly alert to the ploys of the enemy. They must crucify pride – the voice in all of us that wants to take care of our needs, now. The relentless urge that says, "I deserve this, I have a right to be happy, I have a right — to whatever." While separated or in the midst of a divorce is not the time to date, it is a time to rest in one's singleness and let God heal the wounds that have brought about the separation or divorce. Trust God. He is more than capable of meeting those inner longings that have gone unmet while separated.

THE ONLY RIGHT WE HAVE IS TO DO RIGHT

As my wife, Sheryl, profoundly says, "The only right we have is to obey God, DO RIGHT and offer to others the same GRACE God offers us."

Whether a person is outgoing or shy, loud or quiet, don't be fooled by personality or demeanor — our struggle is always ego. It's our ego that stands in the way of God moving in our lives. Someone has profoundly said, *Whenever God moves through you, you've stepped aside and let Him navigate.* Selah.

Listen to the radio. Watch television. The TV guide will say "Paid Programming." Obviously the author of the book or product line is making money or he/she wouldn't be on day after day for weeks on end. What is happening in that 30 to 60 minute timeframe? We're being sold a "self-help" book, CD, or DVD. And in nearly every case it's about improving *your* financial position, *your* looks, *your* health, *your* influence, *your* whatever. It's all about the first three letters in YOUr.

I am not saying these things are necessarily wrong. However, they appeal to the temporal, that which won't mean a hill of beans (as my Dad would say) when we stand before our Creator in eternity. Think about it! God's ways are so different than ours. Everything that has true value (I'm not referencing the hardware store!) cannot be purchased: love, joy, peace, righteousness (forgiveness of sin), and eternal life. The world walks to one cadence and God walks to another. We must be discerning and not be fooled by the rhythm of the world.

THE *ERROR* IN DATING WHILE SEPARATED OR IN THE MIDST OF A DIVORCE

When we're willing to crucify pride, then reconciliation is not only possible, it's probable. In fact, it becomes reality. The error in dating while separated or in the midst of divorce is that a person presumes what the outcome is going to be without letting God work in his/her life and have the final say.

Furthermore, someone other than the husband or wife begins to meet the emotional needs that only the husband or wife should be meeting. The result is a false sense of security and grasp of the situation. The new significant other becomes the only one who understands, the only one who can be trusted. He or she becomes "everything," and the voice of God (whether He's speaking through Bible reading, the pulpit, or friends and family who genuinely care) cannot be heard.

DON'T PLAY GOD

Why would a person return to his/her spouse if someone else is meeting his/her emotional, and in many cases, physical needs? When we play God we interfere with His ultimate plan. This is why in most cases (there are exceptions) I recommend to the person asking, "What should I do — my husband/wife has a girl/boy friend?" to rest in his/her singleness until the other person erases all question. This was the case with Mrs. M.

In this way God can be God without our interference and we don't have to ask the question: "Should I have waited? Should I have tried one more time?" Allow God to remove all ambiguity. Give God a chance to accomplish His work in the heart of the person who is wandering in the desert of sin. Believe me; waiting on God is NEVER wasted time.

From how many people have I heard the heartbreaking words, "I should have never divorced and remarried; I would have been better off with my first wife/husband." When I was in college I remember a study done by Johnson & Johnson (1970). The statistics were as follows: If the first marriage lasts 20 years and ends in divorce, the second will last 10. If there is a third marriage and that ends in divorce, chances are the third will last 5 years. If there is a fourth — that will last 2.5 years. Now, are there exceptions to this statistical pattern? Certainly! But generally speaking this is the pattern of things after divorce.

BOUND UNTIL THE DIVORCE IS FINAL

Most importantly, according to God it is wrong to date while separated or in the midst of a divorce. Follow my thinking here! The reason why it's wrong to steal is because God said "You shall not steal" (Exodus 20:15). The reason why it's wrong to have sex outside of the marriage union is because God said, "You shall not commit fornication/adultery" (Exodus 20:14).

God hasn't given us this commandment because He's some big bully trying to rob us of one of life's joys. (After all, God is the one who invented sex, not Hollywood.) He said no to sex outside of marriage because He loves you, because He knows what is best for us. God knows that the emotions aroused by physical intimacy, no matter what the level, are nothing to play with. In Romans 7:2 we read, "For example, by law a married woman is bound to her husband as long as he is alive, but if her husband dies, she is released from the law of marriage."

A scriptural divorce does the same thing as death (see Chapters 4 and 7); it releases a person to remarry. For example, in Matthew 19:3–5 some Pharisees came to Jesus to test Him and asked:

> "Is it lawful for a man to divorce his wife for any and every reason?" Jesus replied, "Haven't you read, that at the beginning the Creator 'made them male and female,' ... 'For this reason a man will leave his father and mother and be united to his wife, and the two shall become one flesh'? So they are no longer two, but one. Therefore what God has joined together, let man not separate."

If you're at a wedding, most likely you'll hear these words spoken by the minister: "What God has joined together let no one put asunder." Asunder is a fourteenth century word we don't use frequently today that means, "Apart from each other in position."

If we want to get literal here, we could very well interpret this passage to say: You can divorce your spouse, if you want, even if it's not for marital unfaithfulness, but you better not marry again — because if you do, you're an adulterer.

Do you see it? It's not difficult to grasp. I'll have couples say to me, "We just can't get along." "I can't stand him/her." I'll reply, "That's strange, you loved him/her when you courted. Didn't you say 'I do' for better or for worse. Maybe right now it's 'worse' instead of 'better.' What changed?" Inevitably I'll get this response, "I can't stand it when he/she touches me. Yuck!" My response, which I must confess is somewhat acerbic, is: "Well, fine, put him away, but you better not remarry because you'll be living in sin and God won't bless sin."

This is not a gray area. This is not an ambiguous text. It is clear! To date a person who is not your spouse while you're still officially married is wrong, more accurately put — it's sin! God is adamant and clear: you cannot remarry until you're unmarried. Period!

Bottom line, until the law of God and the law of the state (Romans 13:1) have set you free, you don't have any right, lawfully or biblically, to be dating anyone while you're still married. Furthermore, there's no such thing as "no fault" divorce in God's book.

SPIRITUAL AND EMOTIONAL ADULTERY

When a person dates while in the midst of separation or divorce, he/she commits emotional and spiritual adultery. When emotional and spiritual adultery enters a relationship the door of reconciliation is quickly shut; someone other than the husband or wife has now, in practicality (although not legally), become the adulterer's spouse emotionally if not physically.

Recall the words of God in Genesis 2:20: "...for Adam there was no suitable help mate found ... so the LORD God made a woman ... and brought her to the man." If someone other than a spouse is meeting a husband's or wife's needs, the "other person" has hijacked the potential to recreate the love and forgiveness necessary for reconciliation. By putting "another person" in your life you've said, "God, I know better than You" (and you've played God). King David addresses such an attitude in Psalms 36:1–4 when he says:

> "An oracle is within my heart concerning the sinfulness of the wicked: There is no fear of God before his eyes."

Proverbs 8:13 tells us "the fear of the LORD" is to hate evil. Continuing with Psalms 36:

> "For in his own eyes he flatters himself too much to detect or hate his sin. The words of his mouth are wicked and deceitful; he has ceased to be wise and to do good. Even on his bed he plots evil; he commits

himself to a sinful course and does not reject what is wrong."

My observation is, in most cases, these situations are a dead end street. The person who substitutes another for his/her spouse (if there's not immediate repentance) loses everything he/she holds dear — spouse, family, most friends, and, if in the ministry, their calling. It's a tragedy without equal from which many never recover. Thank God for the exceptions!

FORNICATION — A SUBSEQUENT RESPONSE

Too often when emotional and spiritual adultery takes place the subsequent conclusion to this intimacy is fornication. It happens all the time. Here's the scenario — the couple is struggling to keep their marriage. One of them, if not both, is committing spiritual and or emotional adultery. I will ask, "When did sex enter into your relationship?" The guy will be honest and say, "From the first date." The girl turns red and says, "Well, I don't think it was the *first* date."

Here are the facts — when sex has been a part of one's life for years does anyone really believe that when an opposite sex relationship is built with strong emotional and spiritual ties that physical intimacy, in some fashion, is going to be absent? It's the way God made us. The ultimate conclusion to emotional and spiritual intimacy finds completion in the act of sexual oneness. When this takes place, the inner man is marked (in this case because it is outside of the marriage the inner man is scarred). The Bible is clear, "Flee fornication. Every sin which a man may practice is without the body, but he that commits fornication sins against his own body" (1 Corinthians 6:18/ DBT).

As a pastor I see the reality of this transgression over and over again whenever I counsel men and women who have been sexually abused. Those scars are carried for a life time. Another reason why a person shouldn't date while separated or in the midst of a divorce is because it leads to sexual sin, which scars the inner man.

ENTITLEMENT

Here's still another reason — when a person dates while separated or in the midst of a divorce, they often do so because there is feeling of "entitlement." It's a word commonly used today in the political arena, but it is equally apropos here. It means one has "a right, prerogative, privilege, or claim to something." In short, it means, "I deserve it."

For example, a woman has been married for twenty years to a man that's a bum. She says, "You know what? I deserve better than this. I deserve to have somebody who will treat me right and love me the way I want to be loved." In so doing the wife tells God she knows what's best for her, God doesn't know what He's doing, and she has to take control because obviously God isn't. Again, whenever we disobey God, there's a price to pay. Always! I've been there more times than I'd like to admit, as I'm sure you have. We know better than God, we're doing it our way, if God wants to come along for the ride — wonderful. If not, that's okay too. But as the Bible so clearly predicts, when we disobey God it is sin, and the wages of sin is death (Roman 6:23) — one way or another. By the way, it's never worth the exchange. Never! Never!

Furthermore, if you've been in a marriage that's been "hell on earth," doesn't it make sense to rest in the peace of solitude — at least till the dust of divorce has been settled? Wisdom would say: "Don't enter into another relationship while you're in the midst of an emotional seesaw. It's impossible to make rational decisions when everything within you is churning. Rest in Jesus. Let Him be your healer. Let the Prince of Peace be your peace. Wait upon the LORD, yes, wait upon the LORD."

ADD THE LIE

To further complicate things and blur one's vision — add sex. Now it's really difficult, if not impossible, to see clearly. Here's why! Not only is sex outside of marriage a sin, it's a lie. I know that sounds antiquated in an age that treats sex like dessert at the end of a meal, but it's far more than that. When a person who is separated and or in the midst of a divorce adds sex to what they already should not be involved in, it only enlarges and further complicates the emotional and spiritual ties. This driving force is the most deceiving of all ties, and sadly it is a glue that eventually dries out incapable of holding the union together. Therefore it's another divorce. There is a reason why God says to "flee fornication." It's because He LOVES you.

TWO HALVES DON'T MAKE A WHOLE

There is a misconception in relationships that says, "Two halves make a whole." There is nothing further from the truth. In relationships two halves don't make a whole; two "wholes" make a whole. I counsel with couples far too frequently who are emotionally and spiritually "halves." They say, "He/she makes me a whole person." Granted, it sounds wonderful and the husband or wife-to-be loves to hear those words. And although it is true that a man needs a "helpmate" (Genesis 2:18) — I know guys, that's tough for our male egos to take — it's only true to a point, for there is a flaw in thinking that a spouse alone can make a person whole. Reality begs to differ because eventually, the man or woman who is emotionally and spiritually half-a-person will suck the life (juice) out of the other half. Seeking to make himself or herself whole, guarantees there will be nothing left to either half.

Healthy relationships are built when two people, secure in who it is God made them to be, become one. Scripture says, "The two become one flesh." It doesn't say that two halves become one flesh (Genesis 2:23; Mark 10:8; Ephesians 5:31).

LET GOD BE THE PROBLEM SOLVER

In conclusion, I don't say these things to those of you who are dating while separated or in the midst of a divorce to rob you of the emotional or physical pleasure that you believe you need. I write these things because God has said them and He knows what's best for you and loves you more than you love yourself. If you'll listen to His counsel, do right, and give the consequences to Him, then you'll place yourself in the position where God can bring the *right* person into your life should your marriage fail. Who knows, it might just be your former husband or former wife (if he/she has not married), or your separated husband or separated wife. The ANSWER here is: "Let *God* be the problem solver." Why should you worry and fret? If your spouse has been a creep all those years, vengeance is the LORD's, He'll see that you get justice (Proverbs 20:22; Romans 12:19).

How often do I tell women who complain that their husbands are 'creeps', "Don't go looking for someone else, you'll jump out of the frying pan into the fire. Rest in your singleness! If your husband is the kind of creep that you say he is, remember what God did to Nabal, Abigail's wicked husband." If you know the story, Nabal was a wicked and harsh man; in contrast Abigail was a wise, righteous, and faithful woman. God took Nabal out with a heart attack. Here's reality: NO ONE GETS OVER ON GOD; He will always have final say.

One more thought before we move on, the will of God can be seen operating in three dimensions: *permissive* — acceptable but not the best, *perfect* — that's where we should want to be, and *overriding* — usually the result of our stubbornness and not a place in which we want to find ourselves. If we want God's best and His full blessing, then finding and walking in His perfect will should be our heart's desire no matter how difficult it seems to be and do at the time.

What's the moral of the story? Do right and give the consequences to God. You have no better friend than Jesus. Trust Him! He's NEVER lost a battle. Even when you think He's dead, He comes to life!

QUESTIONS

1) In the opening story of this chapter, what did the husband wish he had done that was done by the wife?

2) In the movie, *The Devil's Advocate*, what was Satan's appeal to Kevin Lomax whether he was defending a righteous or unrighteous cause? Has there ever been a time when you've done right and Satan has appealed to your "righteousness" seeking to make what was sacred profane?

3) What is the error in dating while separated or in the midst of a divorce?

4) What is meant by, "Two halves don't make a whole?"

5) After reading this chapter, what question would you ask?

CHAPTER EIGHT

✍

THE COMMAND TO DIVORCE

"IF I STAY IN THIS MARRIAGE
I'M DEAD AND SO ARE MY CHILDREN"

It's been said that every little girl dreams of her knight in shining armor. However, Miss D was not like many of the other girls; she was daddy's little girl and she adored him with passion. She could not imagine loving anyone as much as him.

Beautiful and talented, she grew up liking boys — but she wasn't on the prowl for the man of her dreams. No, this girl epitomized the song, "Girls Just Wanna Have Fun," the typical anthem of a young girl growing up in the 1980s.

Oh, lest I fail to mention, although her father was perfect in her eyes he was humanly flawed; he was an alcoholic. Her family was dysfunctional with a capital D and it was confusing. She struggled to sort out the moments filled with anxiety and pain from the joyous ones.

Sadly, she found solace in drugs and alcohol while remaining disinterested in any kind of committed relationship. She was the heartbreaker and made sure no one would penetrate her heavily guarded heart.

After years of self-destruction, God reached down with a merciful hand and lifted her out of the jaws of death. Soon after leaving rehab she found herself on the steps of the Broadway Theatre (Pitman, NJ). There she was — gaunt, spiked hot-pink hair, and funky clothes. Completing the ensemble was a marvelous song of redemption bursting forth from her heart. It was so refreshing; this was no plaster-of-Paris saint, but someone madly in love with Jesus!

Wisely she did not date. To fill the void she got a dog and poured herself into the call to "fish for men" by evangelizing teens and young adults, singing and sharing her personal testimony. As fulfilling as it was, these biblical disciplines did not erase a traumatic childhood. She was unaware of how serious her own dysfunctions were until she met a man considerably older. He appeared stable, dressed professionally, and had a job with "a title." Was he her father without the dysfunction? Oops! It's not for us to play psychologist, is it? This catch was educated, had knowledge of the Bible, and was focused on Miss D. However, the attraction was an unhealthy obsession, which would raise its ugly head sooner than later. Miss D and Mr. Title ran off to Las Vegas and got married. Elvis walked Miss D down the aisle and Miss D became Mrs. T.

Shortly thereafter the "sooner" revealed itself. Mr. Title was a drug addict.

He said he was clean and sober, but it was all a lie. Four years, and two children later, the now Mrs. T would often come home to a vacant house, an empty checking account, and two beautiful but frightened children grasping onto her legs as soon as she would walk through the doors. In Mrs. T's own words, "If there's such a thing as hell on earth, this had to be it."

As a Christian wife and mother Mrs. T was told by well meaning Christians she had to stay in the marriage and make it work. The stories of abuse, abandonment, fear, and mistrust are too tragic and too long to enumerate. Finally Mrs. T had enough. It was either the marriage and death or divorce and life. After years of seeking God, she believed God gave her license to "get out." Mr. T was neither provider, protector, nor priest of their home. She had no other choice but to assume all three of those roles. Which meant — well, let's get on with the story.

The church she was attending at the time was not the church she attends today; its leadership told her that if she filed for divorce they feared for her soul and those of her children. She felt abandoned, alone, hurt, and confused.

Although her home life was a tornado, her sobriety was strong and steady — nine years clean. It was time to celebrate. What could one glass of wine do? She could handle that with no problem — so she thought. Two years later Mrs. T was admitted to the ICU of a local hospital for attempting suicide!

Not only was Mrs. T dealing with a tumultuous marriage and a church that stood in opposition to her divorce, she was struggling with an abusive and dysfunctional childhood which she had never faced or worked through. She was more than vulnerable to accept the generational sin or, even worse, repeat it. A failed attempt at taking her own life left her defenseless, confused and in the darkest of darkness.

God knew Mrs. T's potential and Satan was not going to win without a fight. Mrs. T may have been in the dark but the God who is light can pierce any darkness no matter how thick it is. He persevered, He pursued, and He loved her in perfect love; a love from which there is no defense. A love that doesn't know what it means to lose. A love that always wins. Yes, a helpless mother lying defenseless in the shadow of death now saw a great light.

Submitting to days of rehabilitation, Mrs. T finally faced her issues. It was a process — much longer than she thought it would be, but the healing began. Strange how dreams missed during childhood often have a way of finding their place in our lives during adulthood. It's a God thing! Mrs. T met her "knight in shining armor." He was no knight in shining armor, just ask him, but to her he was absolutely perfect. On the day they were married her husband presented her with a poem entitled "Can't Hide Precious From Me."

This line beautifully summarizes how God truly cares for His own and longs to make what's ugly beautiful:

Stardust in her trails — she is my long lost fairytale;

If she did not exist — I would still dream her up.

Satan comes to kill, steal, and destroy. He pursued Mrs. T seeking to rob her of God's calling and ruin her testimony! It was a difficult choice — "Live in a marriage that will take my life, my children's lives, and my calling" or divorce and live for Him. Yes, there are times when divorce is right. And this was one of them.

Today Mrs. T is Mrs. D. She and her husband serve in our church, strengthening saints and bringing the lost to Christ. It's absolutely beautiful to watch. In Mrs. D's own words, "He gives beauty for ashes."

GOD COMMANDS DIVORCE

Up front, I know that many people reading this book will take issue with this chapter. Some who believe divorce is *never* right will skip to the next chapter, tune out what is said, or close the cover and shake their heads. If you're one who is tempted to skip to the next chapter, may I strongly encourage you to forbear. Read every word. Put it on the altar. The "command to divorce" — as contradictory as it may seem (since "God hates divorce") — is in actuality His reluctant heart. And that's what we explore in this chapter.

Still others will use this chapter as a way of getting out of a marriage for purposes not in keeping with God's will or in line with His heart, and sadly, will use the Scriptures in this chapter to serve as a means to get what he/she wants: *A way out of the marriage.*

Understand, although this book addresses and discusses divorce, marriage, and remarriage, it does so in the more eternal context of a person's "calling." Remember, when we get to Heaven we will be like the angels, neither marrying nor giving in marriage. (Note: God does not say we'll have no gender, just that we'll not marry. Now, we may not have a gender — that seems really strange since nearly everything in creation has a gender, but Scripture isn't clear so I'll not be dogmatic. I'm just giving you something to think about that's not quite as heavy as marriage, divorce and remarriage.)

Ultimately you and I will answer to God for what He's called us *to be* and what He's called us *to do*. King David is an example we have used throughout this book. In spite of his failures (some would contend that they were many), God summarizes his life with these words: "And David shepherded them [Israel] with integrity of heart; with skillful hands he led them" (Psalms 78:72).

Strange how so many writers and pulpits choose to dissect and broadcast David's failures — as a king, a husband, a father, etc... But that's neither God's report of David nor the summary of his life. God was pleased with David son of Jesse and could not have spoken more highly of him. I can only pray that the LORD would say such kind things about me.

When the servants in Matthew 25:21 stood before their master (the analogy is we are the servant, Christ is our master), the master said, "…Well done, servant, good and faithful, over a few things thou wast faithful, over many things I will set thee; enter into the joy of thy lord" (Young's Literal Translation). We have no greater calling than *to be* and *to do* what God has asked of us. Jesus said that if anything stands in the way of Him being first (Master) it must go; it is a third party.

Jesus makes it clear in Matthew 6:24 "No one can serve two masters. Either he will hate the one and love the other, or he will be devoted to the one and despise the other. You cannot serve both God and Money." What is money here but a master other than God; a third party — something that stands in the way of a person fulfilling his/her calling to be who God has created him/her to be and accomplish.

Paul, likewise, makes this clear in his epistle to the Ephesians:

For we are God's workmanship, created in Christ Jesus to do good works, which God prepared in advance for us to do (Ephesians 2:10).

And that is why, on occasion, God commands divorce. Let's look at it. It is a sad and truly heart wrenching narrative from the Book of Ezra.

While Ezra was praying and confessing, weeping and throwing himself down before the house of God, a large crowd of Israelites — men, women and children — gathered around him. They too wept bitterly. Then Shecaniah son of Jehiel, one of the descendants of

Elam, said to Ezra, "We have been unfaithful to our God by marrying foreign women from the peoples around us. But in spite of this, there is still hope for Israel. Now let us make a covenant before our God to send away all these women and their children, in accordance with the counsel of my lord and of those who fear the commands of our God. Let it be done according to the Law. Rise up; this matter is in your hands. We will support you, so take courage and do it."

So Ezra rose up and put the leading priests and Levites and all Israel under oath to do what had been suggested ... Within the three days, all the men of Judah and Benjamin had gathered in Jerusalem. And on the twentieth day of the ninth month, all the people were sitting in the square before the house of God, greatly distressed by the occasion and because of the rain. Then Ezra the priest stood up and said to them, "You have been unfaithful; you have married foreign women, adding to Israel's guilt. Now make confession to the Lord, the God of your fathers, and do His will. Separate yourselves from the peoples around you and from your foreign wives."

The whole assembly responded with a loud voice: "You are right! We must do as you say. But there are many people here and it is the rainy season; so we cannot stand outside. Besides, this matter cannot be taken care of in a day or two, because we have sinned greatly in this thing. Let our officials act for the whole assembly. Then let everyone in our towns who has married a foreign woman come at a set time, along with the elders and judges of each town, until the fierce anger of our God in this matter is turned away from us." ...

So the exiles did as was proposed. Ezra the priest selected men who were family heads, one from each family division, and all of them designated by name. On the first day of the tenth month they sat down to investigate the cases, and ... finished dealing with all the men who had married foreign women (Ezra 10:1–17).

WHY DID GOD COMMAND DIVORCE IN THIS SITUATION?

1. The purpose of marriage is that two people become one (Genesis 5:2; Matthew 19:5). In this case the husband and wife were not one. They were unequally yoked (Isaiah 52:11; 2 Corinthians 6:14). You had a believer and a heathen raising confused and spiritually bastard children. You had a priest who was a spokesman for Jehovah married to a woman who worshiped gold, silver, wood, and stone whose religious practices fostered idolatry and, in many instances, sexual immorality.

2. The priesthood had lost its sanctification and was polluted by idolatry in both the spiritual and physical sense.

3. These were the spiritual leaders of the land. Theirs was a higher calling. They were leading a nation down the wrong path. It had to be corrected and immediately. These priests had disobeyed the command of God to marry only within their own religion and race. (There were other requirements and restrictions as well — see Leviticus 21). There would be no holy race, godly nation, or beacon of light if the practice of marital infidelity continued.

God's heart was broken and it was time to repent. It was not a pleasant scene. But it had to be, otherwise the calling (priesthood) from whom the Messiah would come would be corrupted and no more. God had to preserve the priesthood. Let us not forget that we, all believers, are a chosen people and a royal priesthood (Deuteronomy 7:6; 1 Peter 2:9).

As is always the case in divorce, everyone in some way becomes a victim — wife, husband, children, in-laws, outlaws, friends, grandparents, and the list goes on. No one escapes. Even when divorce is necessary, as in this situation, everyone is left wounded and in need of God's healing.

ANOTHER ILLUSTRATION OF GOD ORCHESTRATING DIVORCE TO KEEP HIS PURPOSE FROM BEING HIJACKED

How many times have I read the book of Esther? More times than I have fingers. Yet, I've never seen the book, or the opening chapters, in light of the subject of divorce — specifically, the "command to." Clearly, the events in this book, including Vashti's refusal to parade her beauty before King Xerxes, were ordained by the LORD for the purpose of preserving God's chosen people.

One could not deny that Vashti was a person of noble character and refused to be made a "Miss America" before a bunch of drunken congressmen and senators for exploitation purposes. Yet, instead of God honoring her character, she is dethroned. Why? There really is no other conclusion than God's "calling" upon the Jewish people — and it was not to be hijacked. Mordecai, appealing to Esther to go before the King for the salvation of the Jews (even though in so doing it could cost her life) said, "And who knows but that you have come to royal position for such a time as this?" (Esther 4:14b)

Yes, there are times when God commands divorce (or orchestrates divorce) so that a person's "calling/purpose," is not hijacked. In this case it was His own.

TO THOSE OF YOU WHO ARE SINGLE
AND LOOKING TOWARD MARRIAGE

Please hear me! Better yet, hear God, for He makes the same plea (2 Corinthians 6:14): Don't mess with unequally yoked relationships, they are death and break the heart of God. Next to your salvation marriage is the most important decision you will ever make. Be wise. Marry in the will of God. The pain of disobeying God in this matter is never worth it. Never! Don't ever go there. The rule is: "Play with fire and you'll get burned." I plead with you not to get burnt!

NEXT LOGICAL QUESTION

Does Ezra 10 give New Testament believers license to divorce because they are unequally yoked? The Holy Spirit gives us specific instructions concerning this matter in 1 Corinthians 7:8–17:

> Now to the unmarried and the widows I say: It is good for them to stay unmarried, as I am. But if they cannot control themselves, they should marry, for it is better to marry than to burn with passion. [That eliminates most of the unmarried that I know.]
>
> To the married I give this command (not I, but the Lord): A wife must not separate from her husband. But if she does, she must remain unmarried or else be reconciled to her husband. And a husband must not divorce his wife.
>
> To the rest I say this (I, not the Lord): If any brother has a wife who is not a believer and she is willing to live with him, he must not divorce her. And if a woman has a husband who is not a believer and he is willing to live with her, she must not divorce him. For the unbelieving husband has been sanctified through his wife, and the unbelieving wife has been sanctified through

her believing husband. Otherwise your children would be unclean, but as it is, they are holy. [This is a truly encouraging passage for those of you who live in an unequally yoked marriage.]

But if the unbeliever leaves, let him do so. A believing man or woman is not bound in such circumstances; God has called us to live in peace. How do you know, wife, whether you will save your husband? Or, how do you know, husband, whether you will save your wife? Nevertheless, each one should retain the place in life that the Lord assigned to him and to which God has called him. This is the rule I lay down in all the churches.

This is why in Ezra 10 God commanded the priests to divorce their heathen wives. As priests of Jehovah, they could not retain the place in life that God had assigned to them (their calling) while married to wives who compromised and corrupted the command to pass on the teachings of Jehovah to their children's children (Deuteronomy 4:9–10).

Consider this! As you read through the Books of the Kings, note that Scripture is often careful to name the mothers of the sons who took the throne from their dads. What you will find is a strong correlation between the kings who served the LORD and those who did not. In most cases where a king did not serve Jehovah, his mother was not a Hebrew, or did not did not worship Jehovah. The parallel is undeniable. Proverbs 1:8 tells us, "Listen, my son, to your father's instruction and do not forsake your mother's teaching."

Enter "grace" in the New Testament. While God's call upon our lives is to retain the place in life to which the Lord has assigned us and to which God has called us (that's "the calling") we must do so by making every effort to keep our homes intact and free from divorce. Hence, if you are in a marriage where your spouse is a non-believer and it is his/her desire to remain in the marriage, the "believer" must stay and fulfill his/her calling to God and his/her marriage vows. The exception to this would be if the non-believer will not allow the spouse to "retain the place the LORD assigned to him/her."

Let's illustrate by picking something not typical, so that the illustration used doesn't become the final word for EVERY situation. For example, why did Jesus make it a point not to tell the woman at the well (who was married five times) to go back to her first, second, or third husband? Or to marry the man with whom she was living? Could it be that if He did, those in Church leadership would judge every case by how Jesus instructed the woman? We would be focused on the "letter" and not the "heart" (or "spirit") of the law. God's desire is always life and not death; to give us a hope and a future and not despair and harm (Jeremiah 29:11).

It is fairly well-known that the founder of the Methodist church, John Wesley, was married to a person who opposed his calling, not just in the home but in public. (That may be one reason the Reverend Wesley, on occasion, would stand upon 1 Corinthians 7:29: "those who have wives should live as if they had none.") Let's say Mrs. Wesley told the Reverend Wesley that if he wanted to remain married to her he had to leave the ministry; if not she was out of the marriage — filing for divorce."

How must Reverend Wesley respond to such a request? Leave the ministry or stay true to his calling? Let's not lose hold of what "calling" means: it's not just about what we do and where we do it, it's about "being" who God made us and called us to be; it's about becoming more like Him. When we stand before the LORD in eternity, do we really think for a moment, God would buy the: "Sorry LORD, I would have loved to have fulfilled my call to pastor, teach Sunday School, serve society — 'whatever', but to do so would have cost me my marriage." Is God going to buy that? Not for a moment. God's going to hold us responsible for what He's called us to *be and do* — period. Nothing is to stand in the way of that calling. Nothing!

I'm certainly not lessening our responsibility to love and govern our families. We are not unaware of Satan's tactics, and destroying the family is his foremost target. The epistles are full of instructions to men (particularly to those who minister in the Church) relational to their responsibility to provide, protect, and be the priests of their homes. With that said, to our knowledge, all the apostles were married with the exception of St. Paul, yet there is not a single mention of their wives or families (other than Peter's mother-in-law). What God gives us in the Scriptures about the apostles is solely relational to their calling, "Follow Me and I will make you fishers of men."

THE COST OF BEING A DISCIPLE

In Luke when Jesus reiterates the cost of being a disciple He says: "If anyone comes to me and does not hate his father and mother, his wife [spouse] and children, his brothers and sisters — yes, even his own life — he cannot be my disciple" (Luke 14:26).

Agreed, this is strong language, and it's meant to be strong because Jesus wants us to count the cost of being a disciple. What's that cost? Following and obeying Him — period. He must be first. Nothing can stand in the way. Matthew uses the word "more than me" rather than "hate." The word "hate" is used here as a comparison as in the case of Jacob and Esau (Romans 9:13). Therefore Jesus concludes this truth with, "… anyone who does not take up his cross and follow Me is not worthy of Me" (Matthew 10:38). The commentator Dake says, "'God first' is the motto of the Bible."

WHEN YOUR SPOUSE BECOMES YOUR MINISTRY AND IT KEEPS YOU FROM YOUR CALLING — WHAT THEN?

To be completely truthful, I considered not addressing this question directly because of its controversial nature. However, since the *Hijacked Life — Rescue Your Dream* series is about addressing tough subjects head on, that's what we're going to do.

First things first, the primary reason why God permits divorce, and this is my understanding, is because it "hijacks" a person's calling. For example, if God has called Mr. S to pastor but his pastorate/ministry becomes his own wife who is sexually promiscuous, or abandons her responsibility as a mother, all of Mr. S's attention is on "ministering" to her, and his children, and the flock goes unattended. Hence, Mr. S cannot fulfill his calling to shepherd those whom God has entrusted to him. (Please note the reasons listed are things God has identified as sin and Scriptural causes for divorce. I did not name things that are natural to life and may cause your calling to take another pulpit/ face, such as health.)

This is why Scripture requires an "elder" or "overseer" to manage his children and his household well (1 Timothy 3:12). Note, God does not say his children must be perfect examples. It also does not mean every member of his household is serving the LORD. It simply means what it says, the elder/overseer has his house in order and therefore can attend to caring for the people God has placed in his care. If a minister's children had to be 'perfect examples' we would *not* have the Law from the hands of Moses, or the lineage of Christ through the loins of King David, or the evangelistic message of Billy Sunday or Billy Graham, or … and the list goes on.

Adam and Eve had perfect parents (Father, Son, and Holy Spirit) and a perfect environment, and they blew it. God made them in His image, creatures with a free will and they chose to disobey — just as our children, and we, often do. God didn't force them to serve or obey Him; He simply set the house rules. A father or mother cannot live their children's lives for them, but they can see that their home is a place of order and not chaos, a place of life and not death. This is my understanding of what is meant when Scripture says an elder is to have his household in order.

The more I study and put this subject of divorce on the altar of God's heart, I am convinced that the reason why God permits divorce is directly relational to a person fulfilling his/ her calling. Consider this: Wasn't the purpose of Christ's death to forgive all sins (Hebrews 10: 12)? Does He not command us to forgive those who have sinned against us even as He has forgiven us (Matthew 6:12)? Then the allowance for divorce can't be solely about sin, can it? We are called to forgive and forget; to wipe the slate of the repentant transgressor clean.

Ponder the "allowance clause" in the Gospels — "except for fornication" (Matthew 19:9). What is happening when "fornication" is taking place in a marriage? The "two shall become one" is fractured by the adulterous spouse. If a husband or wife abandons his/her spouse, what is happening (Genesis 21; Exodus 21:11; 1 Corinthians 7:15; 1 Timothy 5:8)? The refusal to assume paternal responsibilities fractures "the two shall become one" union. This is why a person with a severe addiction tears apart the marriage union. The spouse's addiction becomes a "third" party and in a much too real sense, adultery is taking place. The adulterous party may not be a female or male, but it's just as destructive because it tears apart trust, robs the home of provision, puts the children in danger, and hinders the transgressed spouse from fulfilling his/her calling to keep God first because the transgressing spouse's "sin" is requiring attention. It hijacks "the call."

IN CONCLUSION

1. God allows (doesn't command) a person to divorce his/her spouse when sexual immorality and abandonment have fractured the one flesh union and consequently hijacked a person's calling.

2. God permits a believer to divorce *after* their non-believing spouse has left.

3. God's ultimate will is to give life and that in abundance (John 10:10). Therefore, wherever reconciliation is possible (and I realize that is not always a reality) this is the path to take because reconciliation leaves far fewer scars and victims and, most importantly, it is God's heart. Consider: "… God was in Christ, reconciling the world unto Himself, not imputing their trespasses unto them; and hath committed unto us the word of reconciliation" (2 Corinthians 5:19).

Over and over again God called Israel to repent and return, but she would not. Therefore, He divorced her. Furthermore, in keeping with His heart and in opposition to the command of Deuteronomy 24:4, the LORD takes her back after He put her away (Isaiah 50:1; 54:6–8). Wow! That's mercy beyond measure.

4. In fact, that's reconciliation in accordance with the Cross. Although God has every right to put us away because of our spiritual infidelity, instead, He calls us to Himself. Romans 5:8 tells us, "But God demonstrates his own love for us in this: While we were still sinners, Christ died for us."

QUESTIONS

1) In the opening story of this chapter, the daughter adored her father and thought he was nothing shy of "perfect." What went wrong and how did it affect the daughter's teen and college years?

2) What two biblical passages confirm that God commands divorce? What is the reason why, in both of these cases, God is commanding divorce?

3) The passage in Ezra that commands divorce reiterates what truth found in chapter 4 of this book? What does 1 Corinthians 7 say about living with a non-believer? Is permission given to divorce, and if so, under what circumstances?

4) What does Jesus mean when He says, "If anyone does not hate his father, mother, wife and children he/she cannot be my disciple?

5) After reading this chapter, what question would you ask?

CHAPTER NINE

⁗

THE WAY OF SALVATION

CONFESSION — GOOD FOR THE SOUL, BAD FOR THE REPUTATION

It's been said that confession is good for the soul but bad for the reputation. That very well may be true, however, my observation is that when a person's confession is offered with the intent to bring honor to God and help others who have been where the "confessor" has been, the good it produces is immeasurable (Psalms 51:13). With all that said, here's my confession.

MY SALVATION EXPERIENCE

I was not quite five years of age. My neighbor, a girl who was my age, had an older sister who had learned some things in school about the birds and the bees from someone other than the classroom teacher. A teacher at heart — I'm being facetious, she decided to use her sister and me to reenact her newly acquired knowledge.

Thank the gracious LORD we were innocent and too young to be affected — physically. However, my soul was deeply troubled and to this day I can recall the moment as if it had been videoed. When I got home I felt so — I don't even know what words to use – wronged, guilty, dirty, shameful, and sinful. Looking back, I really don't know how to describe what I felt other than I knew what we had done was wrong. Strange isn't it that at the tender age of nearly five God's definition for sin can be realized. James 4:17 says, "He that knows to do right and does it not, to him it is sin." Even though at such a young age I didn't understand the consequences of sin, the God in all of us clearly told me what was happening was wrong. Now, could my classmate and I be held responsible for what the older sister had us reenact? Certainly not! My point here is not responsibility — that's a subject in itself. My point is that even children know right from wrong. It is a compass God has placed in EVERYONE, there are no exceptions. Fortunately for me, my nurturing Christian upbringing taught me that when we do wrong there was Jesus who would take care of it for me. Hold that thought. We'll come back to it.

AN ATHEIST ADMITS HE'S A SINNER

In keeping with the thought that "all have sinned and need a Savior," I recall a conversation with an atheist in a judicial court room in Woodbury, NJ. In brief, when he found out I was a preacher he made sport of my faith saying I believed in magic.

Eventually our conversation gave me opportunity to ask him if he had ever done anything wrong. He replied, "By whose standard, certainly not the 'f***ing' Ten Commandments." I think every jaw in the courtroom dropped open. Immediately I prayed within my spirit asking the Holy Spirit how to respond. The man was brilliant and could have easily dismembered me in public debate. And this was pretty close to being public since the entire courtroom had gathered around listening to our conversation.

The LORD gave me what to say (John 14:26). I replied, "Use your own standard: Have you ever done anything wrong?" I must admit I was shocked at his honesty. He responded: "Yes!" I then softly countered, "That's why there's a Jesus." He gave me his business card and said, "You never know, one day I may visit your church."

BACK TO MY STORY

Having literally run into the house I shared with my mother what had happened. My mother gently said, "That's why there's a Jesus." Maybe my response to the atheist was recalled from when I was a child. Yes, just before I turned the ripe old age of five I asked Jesus to forgive me for the wrong I had done and come into my heart. He did. And at that moment I entered into a relationship with the best friend I have ever had. Ever!

That night, at my grandmother's Pilgrim Holiness Church in Turnersville, NJ, I stood up and said, "I'm glad God died on the Cross to save me from sin. I love Him very much! Amen." My Best Friend will be yours, too, if you'll let Him. The reason I remember my testimony word for word is because my mother, Mary H. Sofia, who has now gone to be with her Savior, wrote it down in her Bible.

HOW IS A PERSON SAVED?

For years now I have said, "It's as easy as ABC!" If you're asking "What do you mean by saved?" start here:

1. Do you know for certain that if you were to die you would go to Heaven?

2. Suppose you were to die today and stand before God and He should ask you, "Why should I allow you into Heaven?" What would you say?

If you had trouble answering the first question, you are not alone. Most people are not *certain* they will go to Heaven when they die. They hope but they are not certain. Secondly, most believe they will enter Heaven because they are "good enough."

Nothing could be further from the truth. However, knowing your ABCs will not only guarantee that when you die you will go to Heaven, it will also help you live a life filled with value and purpose, promise and potential as it unfolds in accordance to God's will and eternal plan. What's really cool is that it can happen "in the land of the living" that is, today (Psalms 27:13).

OUCH! THIS FIRST PART IS TOUGH: GOD IS HOLY WE ARE NOT, SO ...

HERE ARE THE ABCS:

A - <u>Admit the truth about yourself</u>

You have done things that are wrong. God calls these wrongs "sin." (We want to call them mistakes.) Therefore, acknowledge that you are a sinner. Romans 3:23 tells us: "For all have sinned and fall short of the glory of God." The subsequent question is:

What is sin? 1) Breaking the law of God, and 2) Failing to do what is required of us by our Creator. James 4:17 tells us, "Therefore, to one who knows the right thing to do, and does not do it, to him it is sin."

Because you are a sinner you cannot *earn* eternal life or a relationship with God. God sees our own efforts to earn righteousness as unacceptable because they are far too often self-serving (Isaiah 64:6).

Ephesians 2:8–9 tells us, "For it is by GRACE you have been saved through faith, AND NOT OF YOURSELVES, it is a gift of God, not of works, least anyone should boast."

This is why Jesus Christ came into the world. If a person could be good enough in him/herself to "earn" salvation there would have been no need for Jesus; all we would need is our own righteousness.

WHY CHRISTIANITY DISTINGUISHES ITSELF FROM ALL OTHER FAITHS

All other faiths but Judeo-Christianity require that a person reach some state of "goodness/righteousness" where "God" will accept him/her. Only in Christianity does God humble Himself, reach down, and meet man at his point of need. And it is here, where Heaven meets earth and eternity meets time, that God offers mankind what mankind could never achieve on its own — holiness! It's the very purpose of the Virgin birth, the Crucifixion, and the Resurrection — God doing for us what we could never do for ourselves. Someone has profoundly said, "All other religions can be spelled with two letters: 'Do!' Only Christianity is spelled with four: 'Done!' How true!"

Bill Hybels, pastor of the renowned Willow Creek Community Church in South Hampton, Illinois, explains it this way:

> "First you've got to realize the difference between religion and Christianity. Religion is spelled 'D-O,' because it consists of the things people do to try to somehow gain God's forgiveness and favor.

But the problem is that you never know when you've done enough. It's like being a salesman who knows he must meet a quota but is never told what it is. You can't be sure you've done enough. Worse yet, the Bible tells us in Romans 3:23 that we never can do enough. We'll always fall short of God's perfect standard.

But thankfully, Christianity is spelled 'D-O-N-E,' which means that what we could never do for ourselves, Christ has already done for us. He lived the perfect life we could never live, and He willingly died on the cross to pay the penalty we owed for our wrongs.

To become a real Christian is to humbly receive God's gift of forgiveness [Jesus Christ] and to follow His leadership. When we do that, He adopts us into His family, and begins to change us from the inside out."

King David in Psalm 32:5 says, "Then I acknowledged my sin to You and did not cover up my iniquity. I said, 'I will confess my transgressions to the LORD' — and You forgave the guilt of my sin." 2 Corinthians 5:21 further emphasizes this truth when the Apostle says, "He [God] made Him [Jesus] who knew no sin to be sin on our behalf, that we might become the righteousness of God in Him [Christ]."

Because of your sin you are separated from God. This means you will go to Hell when you die *unless* you receive God's forgiveness for your sins. Romans 6:23 is clear: "For the wages of sin is death ..."

Let's take a moment and talk about Hell. I am not unaware that to speak of "Hell," other than in the phrase, "What the Hell!" is not exactly vogue in or out of Church circles. However, whether it's vogue or not, in fashion or unfashionable, does not remove the reality of its existence or the reason for which the LORD God created it. If there was no Hell from which we are saved, why a Cross? If when life is over it ended in a grave, from what would sinful man be saved? What's the big deal then! "When it's over it's over." Furthermore, the death of Christ for the purpose of saving sinners (John 19:10) is absolutely ludicrous and makes no sense at all. However, if there is a Hell, and I believe God's word is clear, there is, then the death of a loving God for His creation makes total sense — although unfathomable. I guess that's why John Newton called it "Amazing Grace."

NOW, HERE'S THE GOOD NEWS:

B - Believe these truths about God

1. **God loves you; created you in His image and does not want you or anyone else to perish.** St. Peter tells us the LORD does not want any to perish, but for everyone to come to repentance (2 Peter 3:9). And Romans 5:8 tells us that "God demonstrates His own love toward us, in that while we were yet sinners, Christ died for us."

2. **God is entirely just and must punish sin with death and Hell.** "Yet He does not leave the guilty unpunished," Exodus 34:7 tells us.

3. **God sent His only Son, Jesus, to die on our behalf.** The most famous verse in the Bible tells us this: "For God so loved the world that He gave His one and only Son, that whosoever believes in Him shall not perish but have eternal life" (John 3:16).

Jesus died on the cross to pay the penalty for our sin and He arose from the dead to purchase a place for us in eternity. Jesus told Mary when she wondered why Jesus waited until her brother, Lazarus, had died before arriving on the scene: "I am the resurrection and the life. He who believes in Me, though he may die, he shall live (John 11:25).

4. **Christ offers Salvation and a relationship with the Father as a free gift.** Romans 6:23 tells us, "The *free* gift of God is eternal life in Christ Jesus our Lord." If it's free there is nothing you can do to earn it; however, what you must do is receive it. Which brings us to "C."

HERE'S YOUR PART

C - <u>Commit yourself to God</u>

Receive God's *free gift* by faith. Ephesians 2:8 tells us, "For it is by grace you have been saved through faith and that not of yourselves; it is a gift of God."

Trust God's goodness and not your own. John 1:12 explains, "Yet [even though we are all sinners] to all who received Him, to those who believed in His name, He gave the right to become children of God."

Receive Christ as Lord and Savior. How is a person saved? Here's how (Don't stumble over its simplicity.): "… confess with your mouth 'Jesus is Lord' and believe in your heart that God raised Him from the dead and you will be saved. For it is with your heart that you believe and are justified, and it is with your mouth that you confess and are saved" Romans 10:9–10.

Repent of your sins. Acts 3:19 instructs us to "Repent, then, and turn to God, so that your sins may be wiped out, that times of refreshing may come from the Lord." In other words, be more than sorry; repent (turn from trusting your own righteousness and abide in His). Make a decision to turn from those things that displease God to those that please Him; the difference is LIFE vs. DEATH. Obeying God brings life while disobeying God brings death.

YOU SAY, "I CAN'T CHANGE! I'VE ALREADY TRIED!"

Here's better than good news! When you give your life to Christ, He will give you the strength to change. Philippians 4:13 declares, "I can do all things through Christ who strengthens me." If you could have changed you would have. That's why when you receive Christ, the Holy Spirit quickens your spirit and you become the "temple of God" (Romans 8:16).

In the Old Testament, God the Spirit dwelt between the cherubim over the Ark of the Covenant in the Most Holy place; in the New Testament, our bodies become the temple of God, the Most Holy Place, when we receive Christ (Acts 7:48; Galatians 4:6; Hebrews 10:16–18).

DON'T WAIT!

D - <u>Do it today!</u>

None of us are guaranteed tomorrow. As of this writing three days ago I buried a young man forty years of age. He was one of our Church's interns. I remember the first time he prayed at the pulpit; he took hold of Heaven and brought it down to earth. Today, he is gone. When his mother and father left the casket at the graveside I thought, "This isn't the way it's supposed to be. Children should be burying their parents, not parents buying their children." Then I watched his two lovely daughters, ages ten and fifteen, leave with their mother and the stark reality of death struck me.

James 4:14 tells us, "Why, do you not even know what will happen tomorrow. What is your life? You are a mist that appears for a little while and then vanishes." This is why I encourage you to receive Christ today. Jesus said, "I (Jesus) came that they may have life, and have it more abundantly (John 10:10).

Enter into the joy of salvation now. Don't wait! Say a short prayer that expresses your desire to commit your life to Christ. (Note: the words in this prayer do not save you; rather they demonstrate the desire in your heart. What you believe in your heart is what God hears. God does the "saving.")

PRAY SOMETHING LIKE THIS ...

Father in Heaven, I'm sorry for the things I've done that are wrong: I am a sinner, forgive me. Thank You for loving me and sending your Son, Jesus, to pay the penalty for my sin. Holy Spirit, come into my heart; Jesus, be my Lord and Savior. I give You my life. Amen!"

WELCOME TO THE FAMILY OF GOD!

For you who have just prayed that prayer, you are now a "child of God" and a "citizen of Heaven." These words of our LORD are yours: "I tell you the truth, he who believes has everlasting life" John 6:47.

WHAT'S NEXT?

Now that you have become a Christ follower and God's child, your ultimate goal is to be a disciple – there is a difference. Here are a few ways to get to know your Heavenly Father:

1. **Read God's Word, the Bible.** Simply put, it's God speaking to you.

2. **Pray.** Simply put, this is you speaking to God.

3. **Attend Church.** Find a church where the Bible is taught as God's Word (all of it). God has established the Church as a canopy for those who believe (Hebrews 10:23-25).

4. **Fellowship with other Christians.** Find Christian friends who will help you grow as a disciple (Christ follower). Every believer's calling is simply this: *to become more like Him.* It really is that simple.

5. **Tell others.** Share what God has done for you. Jesus said to His disciples, "You shall be my witnesses" (Acts 1:8). He also told His disciples (and therefore us), "Follow me and I will make you fishers of men" Matthew 4:19. There is no greater joy than sharing your faith.

People will often say to me, "Pastor, I don't have a clue what God wants me to do. Where do I begin to find God's will for my life?" It's not complex; every believer has the same calling: Follow Jesus and He will make you a fisher of men. Note who makes the fisherman! Jesus. We simply need to follow, be sensitive to the Spirit's prompting, and intentional about putting our lines in the water (with bait), and God will make us top notch fishermen.

6. **Give the tithe.** The tithe was *commissioned* before the Law, *commanded* during the Law, *commended* by Jesus during His ministry, and *continued* during the New Testament Church. As confrontational as this may sound, if God doesn't have your wallet, He doesn't have your heart. Jesus said, *"For where your treasure is there your heart will be also."* Note, He did not say, "Where your heart is there your treasure will be also." A person's treasure says everything about where his/her heart is *(Matthew 6:21, Luke 12:34)*. The tithe invests in eternity, prioritizes God in our lives, and places us under the canopy of God's provision.

A FEW FINAL THOUGHTS

Salvation IS NOT:

- in the Church

- in the Sacraments

- in our own goodness

Salvation IS:

- a person, "Jesus the Christ" (Matthew 6:20)

If salvation were in what we could achieve or what the Church could do for us, we would have no need of Jesus; and although the sacraments, the Church, and our good deeds are important for our "fellowship" with God, our "relationship" is in Jesus and Jesus alone. John 14:6 tells us, *"Jesus answered, 'I am the way the truth and the life. No one comes to the Father except through Me.'"*

TELL ME ABOUT YOUR DECISION

I would love to hear about your decision to receive Jesus Christ as your Lord and Savior! Please write, email, or call me today.

<u>Mailing address:</u>
J. Bruce Sofia, *HJL - RYD*,
359 Chapel Heights Rd,
Sewell, NJ 08080
<u>Telephone:</u> 1 (855) HJL-RSCU
<u>E-mail:</u> bruce@hijackedlife.com
Twitter: @brucesofia

QUESTIONS

1) What was it that brought the author, Bruce Sofia, to a saving knowledge of Jesus Christ?

2) What is the one question that must be asked of *every* person, which immediately tells you if that person understands "salvation by grace?"

3) How did the atheist respond to Pastor Bruce when he asked him if he had ever done anything wrong? Why is this question essential to leading a person to Christ?

4) Work through the ABC's of salvation. What is the "D?"

5) After reading this chapter, what question would you ask?

CHAPTER TEN

✍

THE CALLING IN RELATION
TO WHY GOD HATES DIVORCE

In Malachi 2:14–16, God says, "For I hate divorce." Why? Why does God say He hates divorce and yet commands it in Ezra 10?

Granted, if we were to make a list of reasons why we think God would make such a statement, I'm sure we would enumerate more than we'd like to admit. There would be practical reasons like finances, logistics in transporting children, visitation rights, not to mention the emotional price everyone pays who is associated with those getting or going through a divorce. In many cases, especially when children are involved, after the divorce the turmoil continues. As I have said previously, there may be winners in divorce — in some instances it really is a matter of life and death, but EVERYONE is a victim. There are no exceptions that I know of. We could list spiritual reasons too, like "Who is my authority?" In many cases where children are involved the kids have two fathers and two mothers, sometimes even more. It can become completely confusing. I really

133

don't need to catalog these matters do I? For those of you who have gone through a divorce, you very well understand the pain and reasons why God says He hates divorce.

GOD DEFINES LOVE

I believe the foundational reason why God says He hates divorce is because it shatters who He is — love. Listen to God's definition of love. Yes, hear His voice when you read these words:

> [4]Love is patient, love is kind. It does not envy, it does not boast, it is not proud.
>
> [5] It is not rude, it is not self-seeking, it is not easily angered, it keeps no record of wrongs.[6] Love does not delight in evil but rejoices with the truth. [7] It always protects, always trusts, always hopes, always perseveres. [8] Love never fails.[13] And now these three remain: faith, hope and love. But the greatest of these is love (1 Corinthians 13, selected verses).

For divorce to take place one party, if not both, quit loving according to God's definition. Let's reflect upon what love REALLY is:

"Patient" — I love the old English word that today is translated patience, "long-suffering." And in some cases marriage requires a spouse to suffer long, even as God suffers long with our shortcomings. In most cases personalities do not change.

This creates a unique conflict: We marry each other's opposite strengths, which is a good thing, only to go home and live with each other's opposite weaknesses, which usually means "tension." Patience is required by both parties if a marriage is to reach its fullest potential and function in harmony.

"Kind" — What's the opposite of kind? Mean, spiteful, vindictive, etc. Kindness, therefore, is showing tenderness, being benevolent and gracious. It's just the opposite of being mean, cruel and spiteful. There is no room in a marriage for "getting even." That's God's job and He's more than capable of chastising our spouse when he/she is wrong; and, will do a far better job than we. Furthermore, His motives are always pure, ours may not be.

"Does not envy" — This means we want the best for the other person. For example, if a wife makes more money than the husband, the husband is not envious of her, but is delighted for her and in her blessing. It means there is no competition in the relationship, but each person wants the best for the other. How often do we see celebrities marry only to divorce over and over again? Why? Personal careers take precedent. A successful marriage is about two becoming one; the moment that is no longer paramount, trouble is inevitable. It is not 1 + 1 = 2, it's 1 + 1 = 1. In actuality, the ideal marriage is 1+1+1=1 (Husband + Wife + God = One).

"Does not boast, it is not proud" — The Kings James Version uses the word "vaunteth not." To vaunt means to "puff up." It speaks of pride at the core of the action. When marriage is all

about 'me', the "two shall become one" is lost. A prideful spirit has no place in a loving, harmonious relationship.

"Is not rude," does not behave unbecomingly, or "self-seeking" — How often have you heard children speak to their parents 'unbecomingly', that is, rudely and inappropriately? My first thought is, why are they allowed to speak to their mother or father in that tone or like that? Then I overhear a husband or wife talking to their spouse in a rude and unbecoming way and it all makes sense. Do you recall the poem, *Children Learn What They Live*, by Dorothy Law Nolte, Ph. D.? One of the lines reads: "If children live with kindness and consideration, they learn to respect." Rude and self-seeking teaches disrespect. While we're speaking of this poem, let's give all of it our attention — it's worthy of our time.

CHILDREN LEARN WHAT THEY LIVE
By Dorothy Law Nolte, Ph.D.

If children live with criticism, they learn to condemn.

If children live with hostility, they learn to fight.

If children live with fear, they learn to be apprehensive.

If children live with pity, they learn to feel sorry for themselves.

If children live with ridicule, they learn to feel shy.

If children live with jealousy, they learn to feel envy.

If children live with shame, they learn to feel guilty.

If children live with encouragement, they learn confidence.

If children live with tolerance, they learn patience.

If children live with praise, they learn appreciation.

If children live with acceptance, they learn to love.

If children live with approval, they learn to like themselves.

If children live with recognition, they learn it is good to have a goal.

If children live with sharing, they learn generosity.

If children live with honesty, they learn truthfulness.

If children live with fairness, they learn justice.

If children live with kindness and consideration, they learn respect.

If children live with security, they learn to have faith in themselves and in those about them.

If children live with friendliness, they learn the world is a nice place in which to live.

When we are not "self-seeking" we are desiring what is best for the 'other' person.

[Love] is not easily angered, literally, *"provoked"* — I have a friend who thinks I'm the greatest thing this side of Heaven. I tell this person they are "kennel blind." (Kennel blind is a phrase used among professional canine breeders that show their dogs; it references the inability to see the faults in one's own dogs/kennel. In other words, the owner of the kennel thinks his dogs are perfect.) When we truly love, as God loves us, love is somewhat 'kennel blind' in that it puts up with what would not be put up with if we did not love. Dolly Parton and Carl Perkins wrote a song entitled "Family." The lyrics clearly say when we're family our love tolerates what it otherwise wouldn't. As they say in Montana, "You betcha!" The refrain reads:

When it's family, you forgive them for they
know not what they do

When it's family, you accept them,
'cause you have no choice but to

When it's family, they're a mirror of the worst and best in you

And they always put you to the test

And you always try to do your best

And just pray for God to do the rest,

When it's family

Letting go of things that are past, keeps no record of wrongs — Literally, "love does not keep inventory." Now in my humble opinion only God can do this, because only God can forgive and forget. We can forgive, but I'm not so sure we can ever forget. Scripture tells us God remembers our sins no more and separates them as far as the east is from the west (Psalm 103:12). That's divine! However, is it not the same God-quality, through the Holy Spirit, that desires to reign in our lives. We must let Him.

When Jesus forgave you He kept NO record of your wrongs. That's love. When we hold on to the wounds of the past and don't let go of them, the slate is never wiped clean. Love then becomes conditional, and conditional love NEVER makes it past the moment within which it lives. Love that lasts for an eternity "keeps no record of wrongs."

"Does not delight in evil but rejoices with the truth" — Speaking good of one another is a city of refuge. It sets up a wall against the evil forces that seek to tear apart what God has put together. Nothing, other than infidelity, will tear apart a marriage more quickly than putting down your spouse to others, especially family. When a spouse delights in an evil (harmful) report the "two becoming one" is fractured.

Sheryl and I determined early in our marriage that if we were having issues our family and children would not know. That is not to say that we would not seek godly counsel from a pastor or professional counselor, but we would not go to our family. Don't misinterpret what I've just said. I did not say a husband or wife could not ask a family member how to be a better wife or husband, or what to do in certain situations, such as disciplining children, time management, etc. I am speaking about disagreements that are taken out of the home for the purpose of getting someone to side with your point of view.

That carves a canyon between whomever you've told and your spouse. Need the obvious be said: that doesn't support "two becoming one," it tears it apart.

Let's look at this in light of the family. What parents or family members are not, in most cases, going to side with their son, daughter, brother, sister, etc...? Oh, at first the family member may take the side of the spouse who is not their son or daughter, but eventually that will change because when everyone else is gone — there's still family.

As previously stated, usually when a husband or wife speaks ill of the spouse, they do so with the purpose of rallying support for his or her own cause. This belittles, rather than builds up the spouse in the eyes of family, children and friends. It doesn't protect (1 Corinthians 13:7); rather it makes vulnerable the person and the relationship. The aftermath is a chink in the armor, a place where the enemy can shoot his arrows. Keeping a unified front is difficult enough under normal conditions; purposely creating an opening so one person looks good and the other bad only weakens the reality of a strong marriage where love is impregnable, living out God's definition of love.

Verse 7 of 1 Corinthians 13 tells us *"love always protects."* — Certainly, speaking well of one another in truth, being patient, kind, humble, calm headed, unselfish, and forgiving protects the marriage union.

"Always trusts" — An environment that is filled with mistrust devastates a marriage. When a spouse doesn't trust, or won't give trust, a marriage functions in tension and fear. In

chapter 9 we discuss how to respond to infidelity. Even in cases where a husband or wife has been unfaithful, for the marriage to continue and function in some measure of health and strength, trust must be given and reestablished. Past records must be erased, even as God has erased ours. If this cannot be achieved, then most likely divorce is inevitable.

Again, this has everything to do with "the calling." If you live in fear and mistrust it becomes virtually impossible to fulfill your God-given life's call. Your calling will be fixing what YOU will never be able to fix — your spouse. Consequently, your dedication to God's call will be hijacked, because your ministry will be fixing what you cannot fix—your spouse.

Just the other weekend in addressing what man can and cannot fix, I said, "When sin entered the world, by man's own choosing, all the 'uglies' of life came with it. Understand, 'we' can't fix those 'uglies' because they are a sin issue. Science has no power over sin, religion has no power over sin, only the Cross of Jesus has power over sin. e.g.: It's like parents who have a wayward child. They feel guilty, maybe even shame, so they try to fix the child. They empty bank accounts and retirement plans to no avail. Why? No man/woman can ever fix his/her child, his/her spouse, his/her friend, and the list goes on. *The fixing must come from a humbling before God by the person who needs fixing; then God and only God can fix what needs fixing.*"

IT ALL COMES DOWN TO TRUST

The reason why Jesus is my best friend is because I can trust Him. I never doubt that what He wants for me is not what is best for me. Now do I always like His choices? No! But when the sun has set and I look back over my history with the LORD, I can rest in this truth: No one cares about me more than Jesus; no one desires my best more than Jesus; and no one loves me more, pursues me more, perseveres after me more than Jesus. He really is my best friend! And I can trust Him.

"Always perseveres" — Over the years I have given my wife cause to say, "I'm out of here!" There are times when, as she has put it, "I'm last. Everything else comes first in the following pecking order: the church, the ministry, other people, the kids, and then me — if I'm lucky." And, she is too often right.

Now it's not that I don't love my wife more than anything next to God, it's just that I take her for granted. I assume she will always adjust her schedule to mine; that I am the most important part of her life — and mine. Ouch! Did I just say that? Well, as someone profoundly (and recently) said, "Confession is good for the soul but bad for the reputation."

There are times when I have shut her out emotionally and was unaware of it. Our schedules went in opposite directions, which allowed other men and women to occupy my time. The result was that I often poured my emotional life into them. Did I think I was shutting Sheryl out? No. But I was. Husband and or wife, if you are in this same place, don't wait. Correct it NOW. It is dangerous territory. Speak up! Seek help if you must, but don't let it go unattended.

Yes, "love always protects, always *trusts* and always perseveres."

NEVER QUIT COURTING

Make sure you have a date night — a night where it is "just the two of you." No double dating! That doesn't count because the guy will talk to the guy and the girl will talk to the girl. If emotional needs are to be met in a marriage there *must be* regular and consistent times when the husband and wife spend time *alone* free from any interference and distraction. I affectionately call this, *Never quit courting!* By the way, I have never seen a couple lose their marriage to divorce where they have kept God first and dated regularly (never quit courting). If you run this past your mental library, I don't believe you have either. Let's drill it in: *Never quit courting!*

THE NECESSITY OF MEETING EMOTIONAL NEEDS

May we never forget that the key to a truly successful and fulfilling marriage is meeting each other's emotional needs. Every personality (Sanguine, the child who never grows up; the Choleric, the person who takes control; the Melancholy, the analytical person who wants it right; and the Phlegmatic, the person who willingly adapts and avoids confrontation in nearly every form) has an emotional thirst which cries out to be quenched. Every person longs to feel important and needed; there is not a single exception. If you can find one, please tell me.

I speak with female parishioners who, at least in their own minds, are always put down, can never do anything right, and are seldom if ever told: "You look 'lovely' or 'nice' today," "You can do it, I know you can." Strange, but a word from me, their pastor, is just enough to inspire them to keep on keeping on, and in some instances make major changes in their lives — for the better.

I'm thinking of one person in particular who was on medication and in counseling for depression. Her life did a complete 180 all because of a few words of encouragement. She began to read her Bible daily, tithe, serve, and break self-defeating habits. After a year of incorporating these disciplines into her life she was able to get off of the medication for depression. Today she serves faithfully in our adult Bible classes, usher ministry and set design. Yes, it is amazing what a few words of encouragement can do! As the gifted speaker and author, Florence Litteaur, put it: "Words of encouragement are like a silver box with a bow on top." (If that doesn't make sense, I suggest that you read her book *Your Personality Tree*.)

I recall a pro-athlete who attended our church for a number of years, and passed away suddenly in his sleep. On the plane ride home from his funeral, I sat by a person who played on the same team. These words still ring in my head, "All those years of playing sports; all those achievements, this athlete was one of the best, if not the best in his field, and what he really wanted was to hear his dad say, "Great game Mr. W! I was so proud of you, today!" But, he never heard them. So sad! An emotional need that couldn't be met by anyone other than his father — he never heard those words.

Yes, this book is about marriage. With that said, I am convinced that words of encouragement and praise are equal to dating when it comes to keeping a marriage together. For one, it keeps a spouse from looking elsewhere to have their emotional needs met. Praise and encouragement meet emotional needs and build self-esteem while tearing down insecurities. When a person lives with low self-esteem and insecurity, many unhealthy habits form, none of which help solidify a marriage.

Here's still another story. He was fourteen, adopted, and of Middle Eastern descent and appearance. Like oil and water he and his father did not get along. In fact, he didn't have anything nice to say about his dad. He took to me. To him I was his dad — spiritually, in advice and counsel, and a true friend. Mr. M was gifted in many ways. He worked very hard and soon zoomed into celebrity status in his field. Wanting to rid himself of the past, he decided to change his name and asked if he could use my last name. I counseled against it because, at the time, his father was still living. Furthermore, Sheryl and I have two children so the decision would have to have the approval of the entire family.

I'm not sure what their decision would have been; it never came to that. This is what I do know: The reason why Mr. M has propelled to the top of his field and wanted to carry my last name is a profound example of encouragement. I suspect that most people who achieve anything in life do so because someone comes alongside of him/her encouraging them to "keep on keeping on," as Dr J. Gordon Henry would say. It may not be the person from whom you want to hear those words of praise, such as the professional athlete spoken of earlier in this chapter, but someone, somewhere, in God's eternal plan, encourages the person who makes it — whatever the field of work. And a successful marriage is work! So fill the marriage union with words of praise and encouragement.

J. W. von Gothe said, "Correction does much, but encouragement does more." Jim Stovall said, "You need to be aware of what others are doing, applaud their efforts, acknowledge their successes, and encourage them in their pursuits. When we all help one another, everyone wins." Continuing to quote Mr. Stovall, "A word of encouragement during failure is worth more than an hour of praise after success." This remains one of my favorite quotes on the value of encouragement: "One of the commodities in life that most people can't get enough of is compliments. Compliments by their very nature are highly biodegradable and tend to dissolve hours or days after we receive them which is why we can always use another." (Phillis Theroux)

The Apostle Paul writes, "Do not let any unwholesome talk come out of your mouths, but only what is helpful for building others up according to their needs, that it may benefit those who listen" (Ephesians 4;29).

Before we move on — it's important not to confuse flattery with encouragement; there's a difference (Proverbs 6:24; Daniel 11:32; 1 Thessalonians 2:5). Flattery has impure motives, but a few genuine words of encouragement, regularly, can mean life to a person in more ways than we will ever know this side of Heaven.

FOR DIVORCE TO TAKE PLACE ONE PARTY, IF NOT BOTH, QUIT LOVING UNCONDITIONALLY

There is an absolutely beautiful picture of God's unfailing love in direct relation to marriage and divorce in Jeremiah 3. God has put Israel away because of her unfaithfulness. He quotes the law stating because she has married another He cannot take her back (Deuteronomy 24:1–4). Yet, God does take her back. Ponder this unfathomable story of love:

"I thought you would call me 'Father'
and not turn away from following me.
But like a woman unfaithful to her husband,
so you, Israel, have been unfaithful to me,"
declares the Lord.

A cry is heard on the barren heights,
the weeping and pleading of the people of Israel,
because they have perverted their ways
and have forgotten the Lord their God.
"Return, faithless people;
I will cure you of backsliding."
"Yes, we will come to you,
for You are the Lord our God."

GOD'S LOVE *NEVER* FAILS

I am so thankful that God is only bound by His love and holiness. This passage so beautifully illustrates that God's love NEVER fails. Israel, divorced by Jehovah for her waywardness, then divorced by the nations with whom she committed adultery, is taken back by the LORD.

Yet, isn't that what God did for every man, whether Jew or Gentile, through the Cross of Christ? We were estranged, divorced if you please, because of our waywardness. But because God's love does not fail, He provides a way in which we can return to Him. Romans 5:8 tells us, "But God demonstrates His own love for us in this: While we were still sinners, Christ died for us." And 2 Corinthians 5:21 gives us insight into the scope of God's love when it says: "He [God] made Him [Jesus] who knew no sin to be sin on our behalf, that we might become the righteousness of God in Him [Christ Jesus]."

FOR DIVORCE TO TAKE PLACE LOVE
AND TRUST HAVE BEEN FRACTURED

God built a bridge, not a wall, which we can cross. That bridge is the love that never fails. For divorce to take place *love* and *trust* have been fractured. So put it together: bruise love and you crush the heart of God.

WHICH CRUSHED HEART DOES GOD PREFER?

Yes, it is unequivocally true, "God hates divorce."

But there is one thing God hates even more — disobedience to His calling upon a person's life. God divorced Israel because she rejected her calling and her first love. God divorced Esau because he rejected his first-born rights (calling) and his first love.

As I read through the Scriptures there appears to be no greater sin than rejecting what God has asked us to do. God said to Moses, "Speak to the rock;" he struck it. It cost him entrance into the Promised Land (Numbers 20:13). King Saul was told to wait until Samuel the prophet arrived to offer sacrifice; he did not. It cost him the kingdom (1 Samuel 15). I know these scenarios are frightening, but they profoundly substantiate the point made here.

The New Testament's covenant of grace doesn't seem to be as harsh, and certainly softens the effects of "blowing it." Although when Ananias and Sapphira disobeyed and lied to the Holy Spirit, it cost them their lives (Acts 5). A more pleasant and uplifting picture is Demas, Peter, John Mark, and others who blew it, and were granted grace since the gifts and calling of God are "without repentance/irrevocable" (Roman 11:29). The New Testament certainly substantiates that God DOES NOT give us what we deserve (1 Timothy 1:12–16). In fact, that is the clear picture and contrast between Testaments, one speaks what we deserve (OT), the other is God's gift — grace (NT).

With that said, my observation is that the measure to which that calling is fulfilled often changes when a person rejects his/her calling by disobeying God. But, if a person will repent and return, there is always a place for them in ministry. (See Romans, Chapter 14)

Back to those things that stand in the way of our calling, third parties. If anything or anyone stands in the way of God's calling upon our lives, He wants it removed. Now, critical to this "removal" is His timing, but discussion on this topic will have to wait for another time. Let's look at Abraham, the friend of God (James 2:23). God had said, "Leave your country, your people and your father's household and go to the land I will show you" (Genesis 12:1). In obedience, Abraham went, but he took his father with him, which wasn't the deal; Abraham was to leave his father. The narrative seems to indicate that God doesn't speak to Abraham again until his father died (Genesis 11:32).

Still another example is the prophet Balaam who spoke for God. God eventually divorced Balaam because he refused to obey his calling. Yes, divorce crushes the heart of God, but disobeying God's calling crushes His heart even more. Let's look at that again: Yes, divorce crushes the heart of God, but disobeying God's calling crushes His heart more.

Let us not forget we were created to bring God pleasure (Revelation 4:11). It is the very premise of Pastor Rick Warren's book, *The Purpose Driven Life*. When we live in disobedience to God, or someone or something comes in between our obedience to God, this crushes God's heart and interferes with His purpose for our life. This is why divorce crushes God's heart. God made a man and a woman to love one another and have a family that would be trained and established in the ways of God. In this way, from generation to generation, God's ways are taught. As His ways are demonstrated in faith, life and practice, the world sees a Holy and Righteous God. God commanded the Israelites:

"Just make sure you stay alert. Keep close watch over yourselves. Don't forget anything of what you've seen. Don't let your heart wander off. Stay vigilant as long as you live. Teach what you've seen and heard to your children and grandchildren. Teach them to your children. Talk about them wherever you are, sitting at home or walking in the street; talk about them from the time you get up in the morning until you fall into bed at night" (Deuteronomy 4:9; 11:19 MSG).

AN EVEN GREATER EXAMPLE
OF CRUSHING GOD'S HEART

The greatest example of crushing God's heart is when it comes to salvation. Why does a person miss Heaven and go to Hell? Because they refuse to come to the Father, God's way. They reject God's grace, His undeserved favor. Think on this! Although the Law was our schoolmaster condemning mankind by a standard no one was able to keep (Galatians

3:24), in a sense it was grace because God in His mercy and love, through prescribed sacrifices given by Jehovah, atoned for man's sins (Hebrews 9). Even under the Old Covenant man could not earn forgiveness outside of God's way, God's prescribed sacrifices and burnt offering; they too were a gift from God.

In the New Testament, Jesus becomes the final Pascal lamb — God's sacrifice once and for all for all sin, and the only way of achieving forgiveness (John 1:29). It's God calling to EVERY person (2 Peter 3:9; 1 Timothy 2:4). Therefore if a person rejected God's prescribed means of forgiveness (in both the Old and New Testament), that person rejected His voice and calling. What is God's calling? "Follow Me (Christ) and I will make you fishers of men" (Matthew 4:19). That's where every man and woman's calling begins, obeying the voice of our Heavenly Father.

How do we lay hold of the calling God has prepared for us (Jeremiah 21:11)? How do we, sinners by birth (it doesn't take long for our sin-nature to raise its ugly head and identify us for who we really are), have a relationship with a holy God? If it's not yet clear or you've yet to receive Messiah (Jesus) for the forgiveness of sins, reread Chapter 9.

QUESTIONS

1) Why does God hate divorce? If God hates divorce, why does He command it?

2) Review each word used in the definition of *love* found in 1 Corinthians 13. Which of the "love qualities" are presently being demonstrated by your life? Which ones are not?

3) Although it is true, "Children Learn What They Live," why are there exceptions? Can you cite a biblical and personal illustration that refutes Dorothy Law's poem?

4) Explain why "never quit courting" and "meeting emotional needs" are required to have a good marriage?

5) After reading this chapter, what question would you ask?

CHAPTER ELEVEN

~

RESPONDING TO SEXUAL INFIDELITY

FORGIVING YOUR FRIEND FOR
MESSING AROUND WITH YOUR HUSBAND

This is her story: She was just a girl, a cute girl with a petite frame and strawberry blonde hair. She was a working mom, wife, and an acquaintance. She worked with my husband and was the chaplain for the Union where they were members. I thought it harmless when they started carpooling to work together, especially since her husband worked a different shift in the very same company. After all, we were friends and "believers."

Not long after I gave birth to our second child things started to change. My husband began working longer hours and became unusually distant and unresponsive to anything and everything. I questioned him about it frequently, asking if there was something he wanted to share with me. All he could ever say was, "No, I can't."

155

My safe place was always church. That's where my husband and I met and where we could find our way back after we had drifted. He hadn't attended church for a while but was interested in going to the annual picnic. He suggested we invite our "friends" from his work. Great idea! Maybe she could give me some insight about why my husband was so distant lately.

The day of the picnic my husband was noticeably happy and excited. We met our friends at church and during the course of the day things began to unravel. Body language, conversation, smiles, and whispers between him and the 'other' woman were very telling. The church drama team was putting on a show entitled *The First Stone*, and the two of them sat in the same pew as me. They were practically in each other's laps. At one point they both excused themselves and took off to only God knows where. When they didn't return for a long time my blood began to boil.

It's an unforgettable feeling the moment you unmask betrayal by a spouse. A swell from the pit of your stomach rises like a volcano erupting. Your head begins to spin. Emotion flushes your face. Every fiber in your body goes into immediate shock and disbelief.

At first, I fought for him! There was no way this woman was going to "win." Twisted thinking leads you to believe that more sex or better sex will keep him. Sex you don't even want but have because maybe it will keep him in your grip and not in hers.

Then comes the inquisition: "What was she like? Where did they go? How often? Does her husband know?" Details, details, details, I couldn't get enough details. He owed it to me. It all climaxed with confrontation and anger. I decided to physically hurt both of them. I thought maybe a cast iron frying pan when he walked in the door. For her, I would just pull her out of work by her hair and give her a good old-fashioned beating in front of the whole Union. She needed to be shamed and I was the one for the job. I imagined it over and over again.

I began to leave post-it notes around the house for him. Things like "I know" (with expletives). I was becoming a horrible monster. I wanted him to beg for my forgiveness. I wanted him to swear his loyalty. I wanted him to find another job. I wanted him to stop seeing her. He, on the other hand, wanted none of it and threatened it would happen again if I didn't shape up. He wasn't remorseful at all — there was nothing left.

Except Jesus!

I prayed like I have never prayed before. That's what happens when you hit rock bottom; you're forced to look up. Jesus not only healed me, He had a mission for me. He wanted me to give forgiveness to "her." Can you believe it? Her! He instructed me that He loved her too and that my forgiveness would be the bridge that would connect her back to Him. Great idea, I thought, but I can't. "I don't think You understand, God, how this feels." His response: "Yes, I do know betrayal, even unto death."

To say I went immediately and offered her forgiveness would be a lie. Months went by. Then one day I was in a Christian book store and saw a journal with a picture of a bruised man being held up by Christ. It was called "Forgiveness." God told me to buy it for her. I didn't have enough cash on me until I found out it was on sale for exactly what I had in my pocket. (Go figure!) I purchased it and wrote a two page letter in the front to her. Mostly, about God's love for her.

I told the Lord if He wanted this to get there He would have to send someone to help me deliver it. I couldn't do it alone. That morning a dear friend pulled up to my home in her minivan and said, "I don't know why I'm here but God told me to come." I cried. We drove, almost silently to her home.

She answered the door on the first knock. Her head wet; she held a baby in her arms. She was in shock. I told her the LORD sent me. I told her I didn't want to be there. I told her God loved her. She fell to the floor weeping. She grabbed my ankles and cried out, "You are a better woman than I could ever be." I lifted her up and wished her a happy holiday and left. My bitterness, my burden, my anger were gone. It was about two weeks later that she called me asking forgiveness. She repented for flirting with, for touching, for kissing, for — my husband. She itemized everything. I didn't need the details anymore, but she was begging me to let her do this as an act of obedience to God. She quit her job in an effort to work on her marriage and thanked me for not telling her husband. They were getting counseling, she was back in church, and they were going to have another child.

Ironically, it would be my marriage that would end in divorce, but what God had in mind for my future was exceedingly, abundantly more than I could ever imagine.

WOUNDS THAT GO BEYOND
THE SURFACE ISSUES OF LIFE

The subject matter is sensitive and delicate. It is about people and their feelings, about people's hurt and pain. It's about wounds that go beyond the surface issues of life. Some of you, when you have finished reading this chapter, will agree with my thoughts; others of you will disagree. My intention is not to draw a line in the sand and say, "You're either with me or against me." The intent is to lay hold of God's mind in this matter of responding to sexual infidelity so that we all, as the body of Christ, including those of you who are not there (yet), can walk in wholeness. In this way we all contribute to an eternal kingdom and the temporal one in which we live.

This is an observation I have made over my half century of life: A pastor can rebound from practically every kind of failure except one. What is it? Answer: sexual immorality. Why is that? Take thirty seconds and ponder that question and its answer.

Now, I may be wrong, but in my humble opinion, the answer is found in 1 Corinthians 6:13-17:

"...The body is not meant for sexual immorality, but for the Lord, and the Lord for the body. By his power

God raised the Lord from the dead, and he will raise us also. Do you not know that your bodies are members of Christ himself? Shall I then take the members of Christ and unite them with a prostitute? Never! Do you not know that he who unites himself with a prostitute is one with her in body? For it is said, 'The two will become one flesh.' But he who unites himself with the Lord is one with him in spirit."

THE LIE OF SATAN

The lie of Satan is that sex is dessert at the end of a meal. Not true, and it will never be true no matter how the world wants to portray it, or live it. Because that's not how God made us. And whenever we live in opposition to how God made us, there are ramifications — no ifs, ands, or buts. Hear the Apostle Paul's explanation:

> "Flee from sexual immorality. All other sins a man commits are outside his body, but he who sins sexually sins against his own body. [More profoundly "his/her entire constitution"] Do you not know that your body is a temple of the Holy Spirit, who is in you, whom you have received from God? You are not your own; you were bought at a price. Therefore honor God with your body" 1 Corinthians 6:18-20.

Here's the reasoning — when one sins "sexually" the ramifications are far broader and deeper than if one were to sin in other ways. Now, let's not make light of any sin, all sins have ramifications — what one sows, one reaps. That law can't be changed. God set it down in Genesis 1 and even He, who can do whatever He pleases, won't oppose it (Job 23:13; Psalms 115:3).

The popular word used incorrectly today is "Karma." Karma believes everything in the universe is a result of "cause and effect" and precludes the will of an almighty, sovereign God. Abrahamic faiths, in contrast, believe God's purposes prevail over all in spite of "sowing and reaping," because God, in His omnipresence (always present), omniscience (all knowing), and omnipotence (all powerful) can work out all things for His good pleasure, even the wicked for the Day of Judgment (Psalms 33:11; 2 Peter 2:9).

Back to sowing and reaping! When I tell Sheryl I'm leaving the office right now and arrive home one hour and thirty minutes later to what was prepared as a delicious, hot, full course meal, believe me — "my" tardiness will have its consequences.

The reality is Sheryl can, and has, forgiven that transgression many times over, but if I were to be unfaithful to Sheryl, that transgression is far greater in scope because it sins against her entire constitution. It transgresses her inner self not just the time and space in her day. It fractures the vows we said on our wedding day: "I pledge you my love and faith."

What makes the wound of sexual sin so hard to overcome? *It is a sin against who you are not what you did.* To show up late for a meal disrespects Sheryl's time; it is a sin against something she has done, but to be sexually unfaithful is a sin against who she is. It's a sin against the inner man; it's a sin against that which transcends the body and this life. It's a sin against the soul. And it hurts big time. So big that God gives permission to say "It's over. I'm out of here!" That's His permissive will, not necessarily His perfect will as addressed in Chapter 9.

Proverbs 17:22 tells us, "A cheerful heart is good medicine, but a crushed spirit dries up the bones." Proverbs 18:14 declares that, "…a crushed spirit who can bear?" This is the reality of "sexual sin." However, let's pause for a moment and ask ourselves: "Is getting out of this marriage what is best? Is there another solution?"

FINDING HEALING FOR
THE SEXUAL WOUNDS OF INFIDELITY

Because we have those in the congregation who have been, or are currently, in a position where a spouse has been, or is, sexually unfaithful, it is a subject that Sheryl and I have discussed at length. These are my thoughts, and I would like to believe I have the mind of God in this matter.

Forgive and Forget

When sexual infidelity has taken place, if a husband or wife cannot "forgive and forget" to a degree that the relationship can move forward with life, it is better that they leave.

To stay would be to live in an environment that is death. (By forgive and forget, I mean wipe the slate clean and refrain from bringing up the transgression.) No one benefits from an environment that is death; eventually all will die. Death can give way to life, but in this instance death breeds death.

Reestablish Trust

If the husband or wife cannot abandon himself/herself to some level of trust, then there is nothing left upon which to build or sustain the marriage. What was once "one" has been torn apart. I use the word "some" level of trust because trust is something that is earned, so there is a time factor involved here. The transgressor cannot expect the spouse whose trust has been violated to function as if nothing happened. The grieving process, as in the case of losing a loved one, must be worked through: shock, denial, anger, grief, and living in the present. These are necessary steps for adequate healing.

The Issue Is Greater Than Infidelity

Since trust is essential to a healthy marriage, in the case of sexual infidelity, God permits (not commands) the person who cannot trust to divorce. As previously stated, the issue here is greater than sexual infidelity. We have been called to forgive — period (Matthew 6: 12). Divorcing and moving on must be about our calling to "follow Christ." Paul said, "For me to live is Christ" (Philippians 1:12). Furthermore, no husband or wife can fix their spouse. The reality is, the harder we try the worse the situation will become. The only One who can fix any of us is God, and then we have to be willing to let Him. He will not force us to become like Him. Granted, He'll work us over but He won't make us love Him (Proverbs 3:12; Hebrews 12:6). It's a free moral choice.

Husbands are called to be providers, protectors and priests of their homes. Wives are called to be "help meets" (Ephesians 5:23; Genesis 2:18). If these roles are dysfunctional to the point where all of a person's attention is directed to fixing his/her spouse, or correcting a biblically violating condition then the spouse has become that person's God, and divorce is permitted (see Chapters 4, 5, and 7).

However, if the spouse who has been transgressed can find it within himself/herself to forgive and to some degree forget, I believe, it is advantageous to remain in the marriage and seek to rebuild what sin has sought to tear apart.

Is Forgetting Possible?

This is what I mean by "to some degree, forget." First, I'm not sure we humans can totally forget. In fact, I'm not sure it is wise in every instance to totally forget. For instance, if a church were to hire a person who has a history of taking what does not belong to them — stealing, they would be foolish not to be watchful. If the church hires a person whose past had been checkered with drug addiction, they would be foolish not to place that person under care that holds them accountable to staying clean.

However, for a marriage that has been wounded by sexual infidelity to work, the transgressed partner must find within him/herself a measure of forgetfulness. Without forgiveness and a willingness to let go of the wound(s), there is no possible way healing can take place. In fact, the opposite will take place. The spouse who has transgressed will be constantly reminded of what they want to forget and put behind them. If he/she is not allowed to do so, the transgression remains fresh; therefore the wound can never be sutured, leaving little hope for the marriage.

Forgiving Yourself

King David cried in Psalms 32:5, "…the LORD forgave me the guilt of my sin." What was happening here? He could not forgive himself. Marvelously, God came to his rescue. A person must be able to forgive him/herself, and the spouse MUST do everything in their power to get him/her there. If a spouse continues to beat-up the one who has transgressed that is sure defeat. The possibility of the marriage ever making it is gone. The transgressed must, as difficult as it may be, help the spouse find forgiveness. Continuing to remind the spouse of his/her sin is in direct opposition to what God does with our sin. Being Christ-like in times of infidelity, where the spouse desires healing and forgiveness, is what will bring about wholeness to what has been fractured.

Becoming More Like Him

Letting go of the wound is a characteristic of God. Hear what God says about us when we have sinned against Him.

"I, even I, am He who blots out your transgressions, for My own sake, and remembers your sins no more" (Isaiah 43:25).

WHEN IS FORGIVENESS GRANTED?

We are forgiven when we admit our transgression/sin. We are forgiven when we believe we need help — His. We are forgiven when we are willing to turn from our wicked ways (repentance). We are forgiven when we commit to a relationship with Him as the One who can transform our lives.

God can't forgive what we won't give to Him. As long as we retain our self-righteousness there is no forgiveness. And so it is with marriage. For restoration to take place the transgressing party must:

A—Admit his/her guilt;

B—Ask forgiveness and seek help outside of him/herself;

C—Turn from his/her sin and commit to a transformed relationship with their spouse.

If this doesn't happen there is no hope for reconciliation just as there is no hope for our reconciliation with God unless we employ these same steps.

THE BENEFITS OF RECONCILIATION

If the transgressor employs these reconciliatory steps, and the transgressed is willing to be reconciled (we are not God and God knows that so He give us a choice), then everyone benefits when reconciliation takes place. Here are the reasons why:

1. Forgiveness and reconciliation are God's first choice.

2. There are far fewer victims:

   • Children keep the same parental authority.

   • Parents, family, and friends are not placed in the uncomfortable position of choosing allegiance.

3. The return on years of investment is not spent in vain.

4. A person doesn't have to start all over again. Some of you are saying, "I certainly would love the chance!" Don't always be so sure! Seriously, it is not an easy task finding the right lifetime mate. Many of you who are single remind me of that every week when you say, "Pastor, don't you have someone you can introduce me to?"

5. You can grow old together — that's a wonderful gift.

6. You give to others an example to follow and hope that reconciliation is possible.

7. To uphold the covenant of marriage, even through the failure(s), grants a measure of blessing that would otherwise never be realized.

8. You leave a legacy of commitment to children, family, and friends that may not be possible if reconciliation is not achieved.

9. Life reigns in abundance and death is given no place.

THE LORD'S TABLE

When we sit at Table with the Lord and partake of the bread and the wine, it is the very picture of reconciliation. Ponder this! The body of our Lord Jesus was given to mend the broken relationship caused by our sin, if you please — our infidelity. May we all walk in His forgiveness and extend to others the same grace God has extended to us through Jesus the Son of God. 1 Peter 4:8 tells us, "Above all, love each other deeply, because love covers over a multitude of sins."

Reconciliation in marriage is a two way street, just like salvation. God offers reconciliation to every human being, but only those who "receive Him" are the recipients of His grace (John 1:12). For example, if I offend my wife and ask her to forgive me and she does, then we have reconciled. However, if she refuses to forgive me, then we remain estranged and reconciliation does not take place. The same is true of a marriage, it takes two to reconcile. If a husband or wife seeks reconciliation and the spouse wants no part of it, the one seeking to reconcile must not carry the guilt, and neither must the offended party. They should separate peacefully (1 Corinthians 7:15).

QUESTIONS

1) In the opening story of this chapter, the wife who was betrayed by both husband and friend had to find what *God-like* attribute to live a life free of the encumbrances of hatred and vengeance?

2) What makes the wound of sexual infidelity different and deeper than other wounds?

3) The author states that sex outside of marriage is a lie. What does he mean by that statement? Do you agree with the author? If not, why?

4) What are the six steps in finding healing for the wound of sexual infidelity?

5) After reading this chapter, what question would you ask?

CHAPTER TWELVE

❧

HEALING AFTER DIVORCE

SOUL MATES — AND THEN

Their names are fictitious but the story is true. John and Mary knew each other for twenty years. With many things in common, they spent countless hours together and for twelve years were inseparable. John's family absolutely adored Mary. So much so that she was welcome anytime at their southern New Jersey beach house without even a phone call; she could just show up and their home was hers.

Friends would smile and say, "They are exactly alike." Opposites may attract, but not in this case. John and Mary were one and the same, just different genders. Gregarious and high-energy, they loved to entertain friends and friends loved to be around them. They were a delightful couple that looked at life from the positive and made people feel good about themselves.

For the first twelve years of their friendship John would hang out with Mary and her date, and Mary would hang out with John and his date. Often double-dating, John and Mary, with their respective partners, would spend weekends together. It was a camaraderie made in heaven for life. There weren't two better friends on the planet.

One night John stayed at Mary's apartment before departing for LA the next morning. This was not uncommon in their friendship, but on this occasion John left Mary a poem indicating that his feelings for her had changed and he would like to pursue something more romantic. Mary was totally shocked; she never saw it coming. At first she said "no" because she didn't want to risk a long-term friendship that meant the world to her. However, John was persistent and Mary gave in — reluctantly, but willingly. They fell in love fast and hard. "I think I fell first," Mary reflects, "I remember feeling so happy, thinking I'm going to marry my soul mate, my best friend." They had so much in common that it seemed like the compromise required of most relationships was never an issue.

Their history was something they would laugh and reminisce about as they attended church and discussed their own devotional time. Growing in their faith, they grew even closer as a couple. But it didn't stop there, the same interests they shared as friends filled their lives as a couple. They played basketball, football, and tennis together, regularly. They were passionate about the same music, collaborated to write poetry and song lyrics, shared an adventurous spirit, and loved to travel. The two enjoyed children and often acted just like them, the kids, that is. They even loved the same kinds of foods. Their chemistry was absolutely perfect and often had Mary staring at John, thinking, "He's so handsome. I love getting lost in his beauty."

Even their differences complimented each other. She wasn't good at interior design — he was. She was unorganized, even sloppy at times — he wasn't. In fact, John was a "neat freak." But the unconditional love that was the heart of their relationship filled in the infrequent space between them.

So they thought...

Mary's words still echo hauntingly through my soul: "John was a beautiful, kind, loving, expressive, giving, thoughtful, nonjudgmental, exciting, creative, sexual, and spiritual man. I feel so deeply in love with this person." Meet Dr. Jekyll.

As one might expect, when you experience the kind of love John and Mary enjoyed then you do almost anything to keep it even if it means enduring Mr. Hyde at the same time.

Yes, meet Mr. Hyde.

John began to drink.

At social events you couldn't help but notice his drinking wasn't exactly sociable as he outdistanced others who spent time at the bar. Then happy hour moved to the morning as John then began to tip a few *before* work. A few became a few more and then a few too many. The fall was fast and furious and soon he was drinking heavily into the evening and again in the morning.

It was like something had suddenly snapped, leaving Mary to wonder what had happened to Dr. Jekyll. She found herself staring into the cold vacant eyes of Mr. Hyde; a stranger who looked a lot like someone she once knew, someone who once loved her, but now loved alcohol more.

The graveyard spin worsened and John's life staggered out of control. The man everyone once wanted to hire became the man who couldn't keep a job or his driver's license as DUIs piled up one on top of the other. John would miss important events, family gatherings, and dates with Mary. He hid bottles of alcohol throughout the house, the car, the yard — everywhere and anywhere. Mary spent hours searching, finding, and emptying bottles.

Mary now knew; John was an addict. An alcoholic! Dr. Jekyll had become Mr. Hyde. She did everything you're supposed to do when you love and are in love. She would pick John up at bars so he wouldn't drive while under the influence. She got as creative as she could to make sure her family and friends did not know the severity of John's problem. She made excuses to cancel social events so John would not expose his problem to others. She even found herself doing what she swore she'd never do — lying to protect the one she loved. And even more devastating, she was becoming a lie, just like John.

When in public, she found herself drinking his drinks so he wouldn't and substituting his with nonalcoholic versions.

Whoever dreamed this "perfect" relationship would become so twisted.

The once calm and collected John would now burst into fits of rage, destroying cherished and valuable property. The situation deteriorated so badly that Mary actually found herself purchasing a gun; she feared for her life. One day John discovered the hidden gun and threatened Mary, recklessly pointing the loaded weapon at her and blasting a hole in the wall.

Strange how Hyde knew just when to become Jekyll! When Mary had enough, John would get sober. Sounds wonderful doesn't it? But the sad truth is that these short-loved moments awakened all the good memories and feelings, bringing promises of sobriety that would only be broken — again.

When Mary found out she was pregnant, she couldn't believe it. They had been so careful, how could this have happened? She was frightened, and rightly so. He was ecstatic, but not for long. Sensing Mary's depression, John began to drink, again, excessively. However, his problems had escalated to the point where alcohol wasn't enough and he added prescription drugs to the mix. I can still hear Mary's anguished cry as she lamented, "It was then I made the biggest mistake of my life." Mary had an abortion.

The procedure was botched and surgery was needed to correct the damage she suffered because of it. However, it was nothing compared to the mental and emotional surgery needed to heal the pain of sin. Someone has wisely said, "We are free to disobey the LORD, but we are not free to change the consequences of our disobedience."

It took weeks of counseling, but the Christian counselor, tender and patient, finally brought Mary to the place where she believed she was forgiven. Yes, it is a precious place — the altar where God forgives you the guilt of your sin (Psalms 32:5). It's what I (this author) call "forgiving yourself." I've been there, on my face before God saying, "LORD, how could I do that to You — again?" Then His peace floods my soul and I know that the blackboard has been erased.

Doctors would often tell Mary that they could not believe that John was alive — his alcohol level was .4 to .5. As one cop said, "If that were you or me, we'd be looking at wood." Eventually, Mary had to kick John out. No one can imagine the pain she felt, unless you've been there. When you see the person you dearly love on the street, hear him scream, "My wife is a whore, a slut," and see him freezing in the cold with nowhere to go, how can that be put into words? It can't!

After enduring more detox centers than a person could count and having the flickering light of hope snuffed out again and again through repeated relapses, Mary had to do the unthinkable — divorce. It wasn't what she wanted to do, but it was what she had to do. Not just for her, but for him. It was a matter of life or death — for both of them. Mary moved away, a thousand miles away, but under it all she still hoped. Hoped that the divorce would shock John into wanting to change, getting help, and sobering up. Hoped that there would be genuine repentance. Hoped that she could once again rebuild her life and the comforts they once treasured so that when John returned, their house would again be a home.

The years that followed the divorce were no less ugly than the ones that caused it. The day came when Mary had to say, "No contact in any way, shape, or form." Who would have ever dreamed it would come to this? I certainly didn't. I officiated their wedding. I can't tell you the pain I still feel. I had come to love and like John, just as I had come to love and like Mary. Third parties, those things that come in between the one flesh union, whatever shape they take, are nothing less than Satan, killing, stealing, and destroying. I know that Mary still loves John. And I know that John loves Mary. Yet, there is no marriage without trust; it's the cornerstone.

Today Mary has found a new home church thousands of miles from New Jersey. She continues to grow in the LORD. She has tried dating on occasion but nothing comes out of it; the warm glow of her memories with Dr. Jekyll make every other man a shadow. It has been a long and painful journey, but the God who has said "I'll never leave you nor forsake you" has carried Mary to a place of healing. She has a wonderful family that is beautiful and understanding, as well as very supportive in-laws. And like any of us, she still longs for a husband, family, and children.

While I hear from Mary on occasion, I often hear from John. Sadly, he has no life outside of getting sober and it brings me to tears. No one is meant to stagnate; it's not healthy. Mary must move on with or without John. At this point it's without him. I still believe in the depths of Mary's heart she wishes it would be John, but everything tells her if she waits on him she'll be beyond childbearing years and most likely lose many of the dreams God has planted in her heart.

As her Pastor I'm thrilled that Mary has found healing for the wounds that these "third parties," and those who allowed them into their lives, have inflicted. I do want to see Mary fulfill the plan God prepared for her the day she was conceived and impact this world for the better. She certainly has the potential to do so. As for John, he can conquer this destroyer because God has said, "[John, you] can do all things through Christ who strengthens [you]" (Philippians 4:13). Whether John does it with or without Mary isn't the issue at this juncture. It's John choosing life and not death and living the blueprint God drew up for him the day he was conceived. Sadly, at the time of reviewing the Publisher's edits, John did not make it. At least not in this lifetime. I recently officiated his funeral. I'm glad he has no demons to fight where he is today! Indeed, "[God] sent His word, and healed them, and delivered *them* from their destructions/the grave" (Psalm 107:20).

There is healing no matter how severe the wound. How do we know that is true? Look to the Cross — therein you'll find healing for every wound life can inflict. The words, "It is finished," are as real and alive today as the day they pierced the air on that rugged hill just outside of Jerusalem. His work is complete and an empty tomb punctuates this truth. No one needs to remain paralyzed by divorce. The promise of a new tomorrow lies in the Great Physician. Oh, and lest I forget to mention, He's affordable no matter how devastated and bankrupt your state may be. Indeed, this Physician is a shield to all who take refuge in Him. There is life after divorce for He is life.

OPENING THOUGHTS AND
MY PRACTICE OVER THE YEARS

Writing a book is different from crafting a sermon, at least for me. Over the years it has been my practice that when I preach, if I can send home the parishioner with one truth which impacts his/her life for the better, then I have accomplished, with the Holy Spirit's help, what I set out to do..

In most cases my sermons have one main theme (subject); all other points support that theme with the exception of the Holy Ghost detours – and almost every sermon has at least one if not more of those. Strangely enough, in many cases it's the Holy Ghost detours that will make the sermon. Actually, that isn't strange is it? It's like the unexpected save by a goalie during a penalty kill or a shorthanded goal that energizes the team to victory. Dr. Jack Hyles, in addressing homiletics, said, "Every sermon should have a hook." Interestingly enough, I may think the hook in a particular sermon is one thing but the parishioner, because God has something He wants to specifically say to him/her, may see a different hook. But does it really matter as long as the sheep feed?

When writing a book the author has as many pages as necessary to make as many points as he desires, not that there isn't a saturation point — there certainly is, at least for me. However, the reader can put the book down, come back to it, reread a passage, etc. That is not true in the case of a sermon. As to this subject of "healing after divorce," here are four guidelines that, with the Spirit's touch, will hopefully be a balm to those who find themselves looking to heal the wounds that can be, and too often are, inflicted after a divorce.

HERE'S THE *WRAP:*

*W*ork it through.

*R*esolve offences.

*A*ssume responsibility.

*P*ray.

*T*rust God.

FIRST ANTIDOTE — WORK IT THROUGH

Whenever divorce takes place there is a death involved. What once was no longer exists — not just for the husband and wife, but also for the children, parents, family, and friends. What once was "one" is now splintered into at least two if not more pieces. Therefore the same grief process necessary for healing after a person has lost a loved one is necessary in the loss of a marriage.

In actuality, this process can be applied whenever there is a loss or death. I had to do this when our dog Dusky died at nine months of age. We were living in Pleasantville at the time; I was serving as Youth Director at Mt. Pleasant Methodist Church. Dusky was a beautiful cinnamon male Chow with tremendous show ring potential and promise. I thought, "Surely God will use Dusky to help me lead many in the dog show world to a saving knowledge of Christ." I dreamed of being interviewed on TV at the Westminster Dog Show and giving testimony to the God who so loved the world that He gave His only Son so that all who would believe in Him would not perish but have everlasting life (John 3:16). At this point in my life, those plans certainly appeared to be mine and not His. Death has a strange way of making you look at what you thought would be, differently.

My wife and I still attend the Westminster Dog show every year (Madison Square Garden, New York, NY). We take a few days of vacation to enjoy the city and, most importantly, one another. Strange how we can come to love our dogs! Actually, it isn't strange. Think about it! What isn't there to love? They don't talk back. They're the first one to greet us when we come home. (We had a male Chow, Spence, who yelped every time I'd pull into the driveway, and keep yelping until he got a big mushy kiss right on the kisser. I know, it's gross! Even worse was I'd then greet my wife with a kiss. Sorry, those are the facts!

Dogs love you when you're unlovable, nasty, in a bad mood, and the list goes on.)

When Dusky died, I was so convinced that God was going to raise him from the dead. Seriously! I had convinced myself that God wanted to use him for a witness, so I didn't bury him for three days. I would go in the garage where he was lying on a table and pray that God would breathe life back into his body. I know you're thinking, "This guy is nuts!" And I'm not denying that! Just for the record, when I shared this story with the congregation some years ago, I found out that I was not alone in this matter; many others confessed that they had done the same thing when their pet died. It's comforting to know that I'm not the only nut case in the world.

Well, that was a Holy Ghost detour! Or was it a Bruce Sofia detour?

Sometimes these four steps to healing are worked through in the midst of the divorce because it is a long, drawn out process. Other times all of these steps must be worked through after the divorce. Whatever the case, they must be worked through. Here are the steps:

Shock — This couldn't happen to me.

Denial — This didn't happen to me.

Anger — This did happen to me and I'm not happy; in fact, I'm mad as a smacked hornet because I didn't deserve this. (Notice all the "I-s" and "me-s.")

Blame — Not only did this happen to me but somebody is to blame. And, in so many cases, since God is sovereign our finger winds up pointing at Him. (Bad move! You won't heal blaming God. Shifting blame never solves anything. Ask Adam, Eve, or Satan — of course he'll lie to you. No — blaming God only forces open the wound He desires to heal.)

Guilt — If God isn't to blame, then I guess it is my fault. (Even if it is, you can't go back and change it.)

In reality, these six stages (another follows) must be worked through verbally with someone, preferably in person. Seclusion and self-containment are not the answer here. Furthermore, not only are you allowed to verbalize your feelings and cry this out, it's healthy to do so. You're allowed to cry. You're allowed to verbalize your feelings; it's not a sign of weakness. Jesus wept over Jerusalem and Lazarus. Weeping is a part of the healing process when you lose a marriage or have been part of a family that has been shattered by divorce. However, there comes a time when the crying must stop, and that's step six — "reality."

Reality — I must get on with my life. To *keep* crying is to stand still and to stand still for too long will eventually paralyze you beyond the point of no return.

CHERISH THE FOND MEMORIES, LEARN FROM THE UNPLEASANT ONES, AND ADD NEW ONES

In order to heal the emotional hurts accrued after a divorce one must cherish the fond memories, learn from the not-so-fond memories, and add new ones every day. Did not our Lord teach us to pray, "Give us this day our daily bread?" "Yesterday ended last night," as Zig Ziglar would say, "today is a new day" with new possibilities. Let's use today to serve God and our fellowman.

SECOND ANTIDOTE — RESOLVE OFFENSES

Unless you do your part to resolve the offenses from your previous marriage your next relationship, wherever and with whomever, is destined to fail. This goes beyond marriage; unresolved offenses are carried wherever a person goes. For example, have you ever met a person who is angry or bitter? Of course you have; we all have. Do you want to be around them? No! (Well, if you're bitter and angry you might prefer such company because birds of a feather really do flock together. If you enjoy being in the company of the miserable, you may want to do a little self-inventory. It is not a good place to be.) All that to say, I guarantee an angry and bitter person is carrying unresolved offenses.

These offenses could be hidden wounds from childhood, unresolved offenses acquired at home, at school, at church, a shattered love relationship, and the list goes on. Whatever the case, anger and bitterness are wounds and offenses that remain unresolved.

Here's a scenario that illustrates this truth. Let's say that every marriage has one-hundred conflicts which must be resolved for the marriage to stay intact. A couple works out ninety-seven but can't work out the last three. They divorce. When the man/woman enters their next relationship there are one-hundred new issues that must be worked out for that marriage to work — right? Wrong! There are one-hundred plus three, the three from the past carry forward.

Whether you are the spouse, child, family member, or friend, if you have been wounded by a divorce, healing the wound(s) by resolving remaining offenses is an absolute necessity.

One other point in this matter of resolving offenses: If the offense is horizontal, that is, a person-to-person offense, the only way to resolve that offense is person-to-person. No other route will get you there. Person-to-person offenses must be dealt with person-to-person — that means face-to-face. If that is impossible, then telephone is the next best method. Only when there is no other choice should offenses be resolved via email or letter. If at all possible avoid the latter.

Not everyone is a gifted writer like Max Lucado. We do not all adequately express what we want to say in print, consequently words and sentences are misinterpreted, and attitudes projected. When this is the case and no one is present to explain what was meant by the writer, thoughts can be seriously misconstrued and further compound the offense. For instance, the words, "Good day today" can mean the complete opposite depending on the tone and context in which they are said.

Now, you may *not* resolve the offense, that is, the other person may not forgive you if you're the offender, or agree with you if they have been offended. However, more often than not, the wound is healed by the simple act of obedience to the LORD's command to forgive as we have been forgiven (Matthew 18 and Matthew 6:12). Most importantly, remember that you cannot carry the wound and be healed. That's why there's a Cross so that every wound, every offense, can be resolved in Christ Jesus.

THIRD ANTIDOTE — ASSUME RESPONSIBILITY

We live in a culture which, for the most part, teaches the answer to healing is finding someone to blame. "If you can just find someone on whom to pin the blame, you'll be healed." Think this through. Even if someone else is to blame, does it change what you must do with your life? Does it change the fact that you now create your own environment and today you must choose to live in life or death? Paul and Silas sang praises in prison when they were about to lose their heads. They could have sulked, yelled at God, and lamented, "Is this our reward for serving You?" But no, instead, they chose to give what was life-giving — *thankfulness.*

I recently preached a sermon entitled, "Where Was God When?" I received a text from a male parishioner that very day. It read, "Changing the *Why* to a *How* was God inspired and, as such, brilliant! It is amazing how profound something can be and yet one is unable to see it! Thx! Food for thought — your next book: 'Don't Ask *Why* Ask *How!*' Subtitle: God's Expectation of His Followers." The point made in the sermon was this: Asking "why" often takes us nowhere but backwards, whereas asking, "God, how do you want me to respond?" propels us forward.

Granted, if your parents divorced when you were a child you were the victim of circumstances. If you were molested, psychologically and physically abused as a child, again, you were the victim of circumstances. But if you are in your late teens, a single or married adult, in most instances you are now creating much of your own environment. Every day you are given the opportunity to make choices that bring life or death. As a teenager you may not grasp the ramifications of your actions, but that still doesn't negate the fact that more often than not the teen creates much of his/her own environment.

I recall teaching art in middle school while I was working on my Masters in Art Education. The young ladies in the class were becoming aware of the power their maturing bodies had over boys — and men. Did they understand the ramifications? No. Did they understand what it could get them? Yes.

Let's see if this won't help illustrate what I mean. The other day I was listening to a world-renowned Christian radio program. The guest on the program was criticizing his father who is now deceased, and whom I happened to have known, for being too busy when he was a boy. He said he did not get the time from his father other boys his age got because his dad was always on the road doing ministry.

I was ticked!

I thought, *You're right, you didn't have what many other boys had for a father. Your dad could have been an alcoholic, your mother as loose as a "bitch" in heat; you could have had a mother or father whose name you will never know! Instead, for all his faults, your dad married a Christian woman, gave you a Christian home, a Christian heritage, a father with a zeal for God and the ministry. Most kids only pray for what your dad gave to you. Cry baby! And most likely you are in the ministry today because your dad left you that heritage.*

Here's another example: There is a teenager who comes to the adult Wednesday night Guaranteed Christian Growth class. She is fifteen years old. Her parents don't come with her; they drop her off and pick her up. I see her waiting for a ride on Sundays after SPAM (youth small group); another pastor tells me she is a part of the Youth Evangelism Explosion team. Explain that! Explain to me how this young adult, pretty much on her own, without her parents pushing her, chooses to serve God without complaint. Back to the radio program.

On this radio program they were talking about what a lousy father King David was. For the record, God doesn't say David was a lousy father. Did he make mistakes? I'm sure he did. (Hey, God was THE perfect parent and Adam and Eve messed up!) In contrast to David's critics, this is what God said about David:

"For David had done what was right in the eyes of the Lord and had not failed to keep any of the Lord's commands all the days of his life — except in the case of Uriah the Hittite" (1 Kings 15:5).

Would you not say that's a far cry from being a lousy parent? What's the point? Does God ever blame any parent in His Word for how the children turned out? No ! Now some may cite the priest Eli as an example, however, God did not blame Eli for his sons' choices; God punished Eli for not correcting his sons. There is a big difference.

As parents, do we have a responsibility for which we must answer? Yes. Yes. Yes. The requirements for being a Deacon and Overseer make that clear (1 Timothy 3 and Titus 1). And yes, *potentially* every parent is responsible for how his/her child turns out, but *ultimately* each person will give an account of his/her own actions. What's the point? Ultimately when we stand before God, each of us individually will give an account for who we are and what we've done *without* shifting blame.

THE ULTIMATE ANSWER
THE CROSS — GOD'S HEALING

The prophet Isaiah, looking forward to the Cross, says: "… by His stripes/wounds we are healed" (Isaiah 53:5). Psalms 107:20 tells us, "…He [God] sent his word, and healed them, and delivered them from their destructions."

PRAYER AND TRUST —
TWO GENUINE FRIENDS TO HEALING

When Abraham lost his relationship with Hagar and his son Ishmael, what did he do? First, he prayed. After praying he believed that God heard him and waited on God's reply. Now, was he pleased with Jehovah's answer? No! Who wants to send away his own flesh and blood? (Well, I must confess that there were times when our children were teenagers that sending them away didn't sound like such a bad idea.) I'm glad to report that's not true of today. But Abraham had learned that He could trust God; that God always had Abe's best interest at heart.

When we pray and then wait on God's response — that's trust. Jehovah told Abraham, "And as for Ishmael, I have heard you: I will surely bless him; I will make him fruitful and will greatly increase his numbers. He will be the father of twelve rulers, and I will make him into a great nation" (Genesis 17:20).

After Abraham sent Hagar and Ishmael away we have no record that Abraham ever saw either of them again. Isaac and Ishmael may have maintained some type of distant relationship because they were both a part of Abraham's funeral. Now, I'm sure that Abraham continued to pray for Hagar and Ishmael. How could he not? Hagar was the mother of his child and Ishmael was his own flesh and blood, although not the "child of promise."

By obeying God in this command, as painful as it was, Abraham had to *DO RIGHT and give the consequences to God.* The result was God brought healing to Abraham and Sarah's relationship and fulfilled his promise to Abraham concerning Ishmael. It was a win-win.

For healing to take place after divorce, confessing our failure, doing what God tells us to do, then trusting God with the consequences and *not trying to control them* is paramount. Note that Abraham had to entrust the consequences of his divorce from Hagar, and Ishmael's release, to God.

TRANSFORMING THE UGLY INTO BEAUTY

Psalms 32 portrays an especially relevant setting: David has just torn apart the marriage of a young couple; actually he has annihilated it. He is clearly the guilty party. (Although it certainly doesn't appear that Bathsheba gave David a fight.) After being rebuked by Nathan the prophet, King David is genuinely smitten by his sin. A total wreck, David seeks inner healing. His state of anguish is colossal and he cries out these words to God:

"When I kept silent, my bones wasted away ...(Note David wasn't praying — sin often affects prayer life in a negative way.) Then I acknowledged my sin to You and did not cover up my iniquity. I said, "I will confess my transgressions to the Lord"- and You forgave the guilt of my sin. (David couldn't forgive himself, but when he prayed God granted him a miracle of grace — healing.) You are my hiding place; You will protect me from trouble and surround me with songs of deliverance. ... sing, all you who are upright in heart!" (Psalm 32 selected verses)

David prays. Waits on God — that's the trusting part. And, as is the nature of our God, God responds. Now, is there a price to pay? Yes, sin always has its consequences. I'm not speaking of sin in regards to salvation — Jesus died once for ALL sin. We are presented "perfect" (Hebrews 10:14; Colossians 1:22) by Christ to the Father; it is a free gift, which we cannot earn (Ephesians 2:8). I am speaking of the consequences of reaping and sowing while living on planet earth.

As stated earlier, "We are free to disobey God, but we are not free to change the consequences." And David was no exception. However, whenever we appeal to God for mercy and our appeal is about Him and not us, God always responds, working on our behalf.

Meditate on this! David had ten wives. Whom does God choose to place in the line of Messiah? Bathsheba. She is the mother of Solomon. The line of David, the root of Jessie, from the tribe of Judah, is continued through Solomon whose mother was Bathsheba. Now if that's not a work of healing I don't know what is. Let's look closer.

Where is it that you've failed? Was the divorce your fault? Are you the one who broke up another person's marriage? If you'll appeal to God in His name, don't miss the "if" — this isn't about you it's about Him and it's not about your reputation it's about God's — then His healing will be released to you!

Recall the words of David in Psalms 51. He said, "Against Thee only have I sinned." David understood who it was he first and foremost had sinned against. Who it was he inflicted pain upon. To whom it was he gave a black eye. He is genuinely remorseful. He's sorry. He pleads for mercy reminding God that he is but flesh. It's not David's reputation David is jealous for, it's God's. (I am convinced that there are times in my life that I deserve a far greater punishment than what God gives me. Yet, because His name is on the line in that I represent Him, He grants me mercy and is patient in doing so.)

Therefore, God responds in a way none of us would deem possible. He forgives David. He gives David the grace to forgive himself (Psalms 32:5). He blesses his marriage with Bathsheba, conceived in sheer iniquity, and brings forth Messiah from her womb and David's loins — redemption at its zenith. Indeed, it is truly "amazing grace."

If God did all of that for King David, and He's no respecter of persons (Acts 10:34), then He'll do the same for you. If you'll be transparent with Him, appeal to Him for His name's sake, "Do Right" by Him, not trying to control the circumstances but honestly give them to Him — that's trust! Then the same beauty God brought out of David's ugly situation, He will bring out of yours.

What an awesome God we serve!

QUESTIONS

1) In the opening story of this chapter, the couple was first soul-mates then husband and wife. What was it that tore apart the best of friendships and a marriage?

2) The author gives five antidotes for "healing after divorce" to take place. What are they?

3) What are the five grieving steps necessary to "work it through?"

4) One of the main reasons a marriage fails to find healing after the wound of infidelity is "guilt." Meditate/discuss Psalm 32:5. According to Psalm 32:5, healing from guilt can come from only one place, what is it?

5) After reading this chapter, what question would you ask?

CHAPTER THIRTEEN

⮞

THE BLENDED FAMILY — MAKING IT WORK

ONE WIFE BUT REALLY THREE —
AND A FRESH START

He was Jewish. She came from a third generation Christian home. He went to Synagogue on holy days, well, one holy day — Yom Kippur. She went to church every week, usually more than once. He really had no faith; she was steeped in it. He was divorced. Actually, he was the father of three children from two different women; she had never been married. She was adventurous; he was a homebody. She loved to travel everywhere, and did; he was comfortable at home running his three children "wherever."

When his pastor asked him to put into one sentence why he lost his first marriage, he responded: "Me. I was too occupied with my profession, as was my wife. We simply drifted apart."

Christian or no Christian, the parents of the young girl weren't overly thrilled with this relationship. He was considerably older than she, had three children, school loans, and healthy alimonies (which to his credit were arrived at without a court or judge). In fact, the children never had a babysitter; it was either mom or dad. Although her parents thought the man was wonderful and a good compliment for their daughter, he was not their pick. Too much baggage! They did not want their young daughter to inherit three children that were not hers.

One Good Friday she brought him to church. To everyone's amazement, he kept coming. The dad met with him on a couple of occasions and discussed his faith (or lack thereof), the man's interest in his daughter, and what the future held.

It was strange — the man would exit the Church building every Saturday via the Chapel doors and say to the pastor of the Church, "I'm just a boy in a mud puddle." Until … one Saturday he said, "This little boy's been washed clean," and became a Jewish believer in Christ. Now, that's not a dichotomy, in fact, these words still ring in the pastor's head: "My Jewishness made no sense until I became a Christian."

Her parents often heard, "He's only a friend!" But Dad knew differently. And one day her mother heard those dreaded words: "Mom, I messed up — I'm pregnant." The parents were on their faces before God, night and day. "God, what is Your plan here? Is this really of You? Is this Your promise and potential for our daughter?" Ask them. Ask any parent what they learn through a trial of this nature. Again, the "why" looms lofty, but the real question is: "Lord, how do I respond to this situation in a way that pleases You?" But that's still another story.

Well, it's amazing how God makes us find forgiveness for others we would not forgive otherwise if we did not first find it within ourselves to forgive our own flesh and blood. Yes, and at times, as shameful as it is to admit, the thought of saying "abort" entered their minds. But God's voice and the fear of the LORD were far stronger.

"God opens and closes the womb; we must trust Him," the parents would say to one another. "No one but this mature, Jewish man could handle our adventurous and spirited daughter. Maybe this is of God," they would also say.

The couple married in a simple but beautiful ceremony by a lake close to where they met, worked, and were going to live. Today the couple has two lovely boys.

As a Pastor who sees stories like this everyday, I never cease to be amazed at God's sovereignty in these matters. Romans 8:28 does come to life in those willing to let God have His way even in the midst of their screw-ups. Today the parents reflect on God's mercy, and will testify that daughter and son-in-law are a blessing in every sense of the word. As grandparents, how do you put into words the blessing of two grandsons? There are none!

Truly, God works out all things for the good of those who love Him (Genesis 50:20 and Roman 8:28). Now, add this blessing to the picture – all three of the husband's children from his previous relationships have received Christ. At the time of this writing, I had the privilege of praying with the youngest who received the LORD in Sunday School, and came to the Chapel to witness what he had done. I literally had to choke back the tears; I never cease to be amazed at God's immeasurable love.

Today the parents of the young girl stand on Proverbs 22:6 as they watch their two grandsons grow up being trained in the way of the LORD, rejoicing everyday in the son-in-law with whom the LORD has blessed them.

He's bright, well versed at his profession, an excellent and interesting writer (although that is not his profession) and a wonderful and loving husband and father. Furthermore, he's a man who has matured in his Christian faith far beyond those who have been saved for many more years than he. As one writer put it: "When twenty-five years go by [some people] don't gain twenty-five years' experience, they gain one year of experience twenty-five times! To win in life you must turn your experience into wisdom." The same is true of our walk with Christ.

Yes, the consequences of divorce remain — recall one of our premises: Not all divorce is sin, but what leads to it is. And, as is the nature of our God, He specializes in making the ugly beautiful. For those who have been divorced — right or wrong, innocent or guilty, if you will surrender your failure to God in honesty, ask the LORD for divine intervention, listen to what He tells you as directed by His Word and Spirit, He will find a plus in your pile of minuses. And that's a guarantee — not mine, but His.

THE QUESTION: WAS DIVORCE RIGHT IN THIS INSTANCE?

Let me echo the words of a dear Jewish friend, "Let's be Jewish and answer a question with a question." Is making a mess and turning it into something beautiful right? Years ago, more than I'd like to recount, I heard Zig Ziglar at a John Maxwell pastors' conference in San Diego, California. I will always remember his words as he summarized the hope of Christianity with this statement (which I quoted earlier): "Yesterday ended last night, today's a new day."

Is divorce right? Sometimes. Most of the time, no. Yet, when God chooses to take the natural and transform it with the supernatural He makes the wrong right. That's what happened in the above story, which is what God also does in salvation. He takes upon Himself our transgressions so that we can be seen "blameless" (Colossians 1:22; 2 Corinthians 5:21). Truly, His grace is "amazing."

I love the way Henry Smith, the 19th Century theologian, poignantly put it: "He hides our <u>un</u>righteousness with His righteousness; He covers our <u>dis</u>obedience with His obedience;

He shadows <u>our death</u> with His death [so] that the wrath of God cannot find us."

As the Psalmist would say, "Selah."

In Genesis 12 God calls Abram, later to be named Abraham, to follow Him. He tells Abraham that He will make of him a great nation, blessing those who bless Abraham, and cursing those who curse Abraham. Indeed history has revealed this to be true. He also tells Abraham that through him, that is his seed, all nations will be blessed.

In Genesis 16, Abraham is eight-five years old and Sarah, his wife, is seventy-five. They have no children. Sarah is becoming impatient and makes a suggestion: Why not use a surrogate mother? Abraham decides to go with the suggestion and the rest is history — so to speak!

Abraham slept with Hagar, Sarah's maidservant; she became pregnant and gave birth to a male child whom they name Ishmael, which means "God hears."

AN INTERESTING SIDE NOTE RELATIONAL TO ISHMAEL, CURRENT EVENTS, AND HISTORY

Listen to what says God about this male child in Genesis 16:11-12:

"The angel of the LORD also said to her [Hagar, who is fleeing from Sarah because she has been mistreated by Sarah, but not without cause]:'You are now with child and you will have a son. You shall name him Ishmael, for the LORD has heard of your misery. He will be a wild donkey of a man; his hand will be against everyone and everyone's hand against him, and he will live in hostility toward all his brothers'."

And to this day the non-Christian Arab community lives in hostility with ALL of its brothers. Cut through the political rhetoric! There is only one way that peace will come to the Middle East and that's through Jesus Christ. And if it is to come now, it can only come if nationalities will be one in Him. Galatians 3:28 tells us "There is neither Jew nor Greek, slave nor free, male nor female, for you are all one in Christ Jesus."

Without question, peace will come when Jesus returns to Earth and sets up his Millennial reign. Whatever the case, God's Word cannot lie and will continue to disprove the vain assertions of all skeptics. With that in mind, let's return to Genesis and the blended family.

GOD'S PROMISE TO BLESS ABRAHAM AND HIS SEED

In Genesis 17:20, the LORD tells Abraham, "And as for Ishmael, I have heard you: I will surely bless him." What is happening here? Abraham is torn apart by this blended family. Ishmael is his son. Sarah is his wife. The mother of Ishmael is still living in his house. Sarah dislikes Hagar (Ishmael's mother). Ishmael has never become Sarah's child. If anything, he has created a bond between Hagar and Abraham that was not there prior to his birth, and driven a wedge between Abraham and Sarah. This is not a family of happy campers, literally. (Remember they were tent dwellers.)

God continues speaking to Abraham and tells him: "I will make him [Ishmael] fruitful and will greatly increase his numbers. He will be the father of twelve rulers, and I will make him into a great nation."

When Abraham is one hundred years old and Sarah is ninety years old, God gives them the "son of promise," Isaac. Now we have a fully blended or merged family: two mothers, two children, one by each mom, same dad. And sparks begin to fly. Some of you are saying, "Been there!"

MARRIED AND LIVING IN TWO DIFFERENT HOUSES

It has been my observation over the years that if a second marriage struggles, it is more often than not related to the children. In most cases the divorced father/mother feels guilty and subsequently tends to be more lenient towards his/her child than he/she should. This does not go unnoticed by the spouse (now husband or wife). Being more objective and therefore less tolerant, this frequently creates tension and disagreement between the husband and wife. Where there are two sets of children merging, the problems only enhance.

This story is almost comical, but it does propose a solution where no other resolution has been found. Recently, we had a family in the church merge families with three sets of children — all of whom were teenagers. Need I say anymore? There is constant disagreement among the children, and neither newlywed can agree on a solution. So, his children live with him in his home and her children live with her in her home. I suspect that is how kings survived blended family situations where there were many wives and children. I sincerely doubt that they all lived in the same house. (If you recall, King David had ten wives and nineteen sons. Now that's a blended family!)

Don't misunderstand, I am not recommending this as a solution to making a blended family work. However, if the solution works until the teens are on their own or in college, it is certainly better than another divorce. Ideally both should sell their houses, buy one home, and start anew. For a marriage to work the "two must become one," (Mark 10:8) and that doesn't mean only in the bedroom. His and hers must become "ours;" that's when a house becomes a home. This is why Jesus said, "… it was not this way from the beginning," referencing more than one wife (Matthew 19:8). The plan was one man and one wife, till death parts them (Romans 7:2; 1 Corinthians 7:39).

FOR THE SECOND MARRIAGE TO WORK

For the second or third marriage to work there must be a commitment on the part of the husband and wife to make each other first priority, not the children. When you said your vows before God they did not say, "I take my son/daughter to be my soul mate. I am one flesh with my son/daughter." Children are raised to be fledged! (Fledged is a word used for when the adult birds push their maturing young out of the nest so they learn to fly and feed on their own.) There comes a time when son or daughter leaves mother and father and cleaves to his wife/her husband and the two become one flesh. The child is now one flesh with the spouse, not with the parents. We'll come back to this shortly.

Back to the story of Abraham and Sarah (Genesis 21):

4 When his son Isaac was eight days old, Abraham circumcised him, as God commanded him. ... 6 Sarah said, ... 7 "Who would have said ... Sarah would nurse children? ...Yet I have borne [Abraham] a son in his old age." 8 The child grew and was weaned, and on the day Isaac was weaned Abraham held a great feast. 9 But Sarah saw that the son whom Hagar the Egyptian had borne to Abraham was mocking, 10 and she said to Abraham, "Get rid of that slave woman and her son, for that slave woman's son will never share in the inheritance with my son Isaac." [Ishmael was fourteen years old.]

11 The matter distressed Abraham greatly because it concerned his son. 12 But God said to him, "Do not be so distressed about the boy and your maidservant. Listen to whatever Sarah tells you, because it is through Isaac that your offspring will be reckoned. 13 I will make the son of the maidservant into a nation also, because he is your offspring."

14 Early the next morning Abraham took some food and a skin of water and gave them to Hagar. He set them on her shoulders and then sent her off with the boy. …

20 God was with the boy as he grew up. He lived in the desert and became an archer. 21 While he was living in the Desert of Paran, his mother got a wife for him from Egypt.

THE SPOUSE MUST BE FIRST

One simple and profound truth is implied by this narrative: if a marriage is to be successful the spouse must be first, not children, not hobby, not job, not internet, not parent-s, but the husband and/or wife. Only God can supersede a spouse in priority. When Ishmael came between Abraham and Sarah, God in essence said to Abraham, "Your allegiance is to your wife, Sarah, and your call is to be fulfilled through the child born to your wife, not Ishmael, the son of the surrogate mother."

Ponder this carefully — I am *not* saying that a parent's allegiance should not be with the children after a divorce. What I am saying is, if a man or woman remarries, for that marriage to work his/her allegiance must be to the spouse first, not the children. For a marriage to work the way God intended it to work, the husband and wife must be one with each other; no other can put that relationship asunder, not even children.

Scripture makes it clear: "… the two shall become one flesh" (Matthew 19:5). The priority, the allegiance must be to the spouse. If you cannot put the spouse first then don't even consider remarriage. It's not an option. If the spouse is not first, you've written a guarantee for an unfulfilled relationship, if not failure.

A single or separated parent may say, "My allegiance is to my children," and that certainly is a mother or father's right to put a child first. In fact, in some cases it may be the only option, at least for a season of time. However, if this is the case, then don't remarry; because the moment you remarry your biblical allegiance is first to your spouse, then to the children.

HEALTHY DISCUSSIONS

Because my wife, Sheryl, and I deal with these matters on a pretty regular basis, topics such as these are discussed often. She has sacrificially given to me, and the work to which I have been called, and says categorically, "That's why, if something happened to you, I would never remarry — my children would come first. That's just the way it would be."

Now if something really did happen to me (Lord, may that not be! I would like to think I have a few, if not many, good years left.) I would like her to reconsider. I really would. I would not want her to spend the rest of her years alone. But she says, "Never!" I tell her, "Some rich Aristotle Onassis will come along wooing you with a huge bank account, diamonds, yachts, and sweet talk, and it will be all over." Of course she denies it but I know it will be, "Bruce who?"

Actually, I used to believe that, but as we grow older together, we'll be married thirty-eight years at this writing, I believe she would not remarry and that the kids and grandchildren would be her spouse, figuratively speaking.

PRESCRIPTIONS FOR SUCCESS

For a number of years we ran marriage seminars for couples preparing for marriage. Today we handle these sessions individually, pastor and couple. One of the sessions was "The Blended Family." It was taught by Rev. Robert S. Barber, better known to all of us as Pastor Bob. Today Pastor Bob is the school headmaster of Bethel Prep Classical Christian Academy, and has a Doctorate in Education/Leadership Development.

Pastor Bob entered the ministry as a single parent with custody of both his children. While pastoring a church in a neighboring town, he would come to some of our singles ministry activities and, there, met one of the lovely young ladies who also worked in our office. A few years later they married, and as God would have it, had children and a "blended family." Annmarie, his lovely wife, became a mother to the two children they would have together and the two she would raise, in part, as her own.

Pastor Bob has graciously granted me permission to use his outline "Blended Families and Raising Children of Promise." The illustrations are mine.

FIRST THINGS FIRST

If you don't want another failed marriage, you must begin by recognizing:

THE STAGES OF BLENDED-FAMILY ADJUSTMENTS

Fantasy Stage *(Unrealistic Expectations)*

For a blended family to be successful one must guard against the dream of gaining happiness and wholeness through a new marriage. There are many dreams — not that these are wrong — they just tend to be unrealistic. Here are some of them:

- I won't make the same mistakes as in my first marriage.

- My new spouse will love my children.

- I will love my spouse's children as my much as I do my own.

- This new love is enough to conquer any problem we will face.

Factual Stage *(Reality Sets In)*

- A unified family life may not be reality. Everyone in my family may not see my new husband/wife the same way I do.

- The guilt, jealousy, and anger from former relationships are damaging to the new relationships.

- The children are mourning their lost parent and not accepting the stepparent. In some instances children are not only adjusting to a new parent (stepdad or mother), but they are feeling like they've just lost a father or mother (you). Need I say here that the emotions a child or teen feels in these situations are extremely volatile and often expressed via a poor attitude at school and home? An "A" student can easily go to being a non-caring student. Parents in these situations must be understanding, nonjudgmental, and open to listening even if what is said hurts. But they should not accept disrespectful behavior.

- The transition of a new family becomes more difficult than expected.

- The problems seem too difficult and many times there is a strong temptation to give up.

Fruitful Stage *(Growth and Maturity)*

- The realization that a blended family is not ideal; there will most likely always be a unique set of family problems.

- The realization that mistakes will be made, but God uses mistakes to build character and strengthen the family unit.

- The realization that it is going to take the intentional cooperation of both partners to overcome difficulties and make the marriage work.

- The realization that it takes time, maybe even years, before there are any signs of unity or true acceptance.

- The realization that God will use this blended family as a source of spiritual growth, a means of healing the past, and a demonstration of His unconditional love.

SECOND THINGS FIRST!

If you don't want another failed marriage you must begin by recognizing:

ISSUES SURROUNDING STEP-FAMILIES

Loss

- All members are dealing with the loss of the nuclear (first marriage) family.

- Children are grieving the loss of a parent.

- Spouses are grieving the loss of significant relationships.

Fear

- Children fear the loss of affection.

- Children fear the unknown.

- Children fear rejection.

- Children fear unfair treatment.

- Spouses fear a second failure.

- Stepparents fear rejection.

Anger

- Over lack of acceptance.

- Over lack of or too much discipline.

- Over financial commitments and the added stress due to the additional responsibility. Divorce too often victimizes both parties' financial positions.

- Over unfulfilled expectations, dreams, and goals.

Guilt

- Children feel guilty over divided loyalties.

- Children feel guilty thinking they are responsible for the failure of the first marriage.

- Children feel guilty about not accepting and loving the stepparent.

- Spouse feels guilty because of his/her divorce and its affect on the children.

- Spouse feels guilty over giving priority to bonding with the new spouse.

- Spouse feels guilty over not loving the stepchildren as his/her own.

LAST BUT FIRST! REAL AND NECESSARY ESSENTIALS TO A SUCCESSFUL SECOND MARRIAGE

If you don't want another failed marriage you must begin by:

OVERCOMING THE PAST

Ask yourself, "Where did I sin?" and "Where was I sinned against?" (1 John 1:9; Matthew 6:15)

In the first case, ask God and your former spouse for forgiveness. In the latter case, forgive your spouse. Jesus said, "Forgive us our debts as we forgive our debtors" (Matthew 6:12). Slates must be wiped clean if a new start is to succeed.

BUILD ON A FIRM FOUNDATION

Keep the relationship holy (Psalms 37:4; 1 Peter 2:9) and strive to meet the needs of your spouse (Romans 5:8).

Nothing will crack a foundation faster than mistrust. Stay true and demonstrate to your spouse, through words and actions, that they are valued, trusted and loved. Nothing is more important to our spouses than letting them know that they are valued and important. When a spouse feels like anyone can do what he/she is doing, emotional bonding is lost and emotional needs look to be met elsewhere — children, family, friends, and even strangers. This is a huge yellow flag waving in the wind.

MY PERSONAL REFLECTIONS

I can easily put in six fourteen-hour days. Our oldest child, Joel, would, as a small boy, often give me a priority balance check. We'd have finished supper, and I'd be leaving the house, usually for something related to church life. Joel would stand peering through the glass storm door and say to Sheryl, "When is daddy coming home?"

Sheryl was even more direct. When she was frustrated, overwhelmed, and felt used (which wasn't often — she's got a pretty strong constitution), she would say, "Anybody can do what I do — prepare your meals, do the laundry, keep the house clean, and grant you sexual favors. I'm nothing but a hired hand!"

It isn't often I hear those words, much less now than then, but when I do, I know that she's had enough. And, she's right. Women and men need to feel valuable, and nothing expresses that more than the place and time we give to our spouses. Words, although important, can sound pretty hallow if they are not backed up with action.

BUILD THE RELATIONSHIP TO LAST

Invest in one another. There's no return where nothing has been deposited; there's no harvest if nothing has been planted. Invest for the long haul; marriage is meant to last for a lifetime.

The strongest message you can send to your children and those around you is what you invest in one another. How you respect each other and treat each other will trump anything you say. Love is an action not a feeling; it's commanded not optional, it's giving not getting; and it's costly not free (Genesis 2:24; Ephesians 5:31–32). How many children have we seen graduate from a religious private school, be involved in their church youth group only to drift as soon as they reach their adult years. After some investigation the truth becomes evident, their home was a façade. What they learned in Christian school and youth group was not what they heard or saw at home, and the collision of messages hit them like a sucker-punch that sent them sprawling to the canvas.

Hopefully, the Word planted in their early and teen years has not been plucked up by the ravens and scorched by the sun, but eventually will take root and flourish.

Investing in our children and helping them discover and pursue God's purposes for their lives (Ephesians 2:10) through Christian education and the church is noble and encouraged, but living the gospel transparently without hypocrisy is by far the greatest foundation any parent can give his/her children

THE FAMILY ALTAR

When our children were small we made it a point to have "Family Altar" every evening. I may have been out all day and then again at night, but I did my best to be home for dinner. During our Family Altar I would read something from the Bible or something that referenced the Bible as our final authority for life, faith and the practice thereof. We would look at life from God's perspective and how that differed from the world's view, and why God's ways were life and the world's ways were death. We would ask our children for their input and then take prayer requests.

The times were precious and have impacted our children for eternity. It's been said that what children learn by the age of seven is what they will return to as an adult. The only exception to that proverb is when a person becomes a "new creation" through spiritual birth (1 Corinthians 5:17).

FINAL THOUGHTS

God called Abraham, a Chaldean, out of a heathen country and sanctified (separated) him unto Himself. He and his family from that time forth became a chosen people. That's the biblical definition of a church, "a called out people; a fellowship" (fellows in the same ship).

When Messiah comes He grafts into Abraham's family ALL who believe and come to the Father via the Cross of Christ. Jesus said, "He that believes in the Son has everlasting life; and he who does not believe the Son does not have life" (John 3:36). Saint Paul tells the Galatians: Consider Abraham: "He believed God, and it was credited to him as righteousness." Understand, then, that those who believe are children of Abraham. (Galatians 3:6-7).

In Romans 11:17 Paul speaks about the Gentiles being "grafted in." What does that mean? Both Jew and non-Jew are ONE family. So in a sense, a real sense, we who are not Jews are Jews because Messiah has placed us into his family. As a blended family we who are not Jews are no longer outsiders. Why? Because we have the same Father. Saint Peter put it this way: "… you are a chosen people, a royal priesthood, a holy nation, a people belonging to God, that you may declare the praises of Him who called you out of darkness into His wonderful light" (1 Peter 2:9).

So, what's all that theology jargon about? Let's simplify it: If God by His grace can make a blended family (Jew and

Gentile) successful, then by His grace so can we (Philippians 4:13). As we would say in south Jersey jargon, "Cool!"

QUESTIONS

1) In the opening story of this chapter, the Pastor asked the husband why he lost his first marriage. What was the man's response? If you are in a second, or more, marriage, what would you say is the reason why you lost your marriage?

2) In what way was Abraham's marriage similar to the blended family of today?

3) The author is adamant about 'the spouse' being first (not the children), for a marriage to work. Why does he espouse that maxim? Do you agree? Why? Why not?

4) Name the three components necessary for a blended family to succeed.

5) After reading this chapter, what question would you ask?

CHAPTER FOURTEEN

❧

TRUSTING GOD

TRUSTING GOD WHEN
EVERYTHING SAYS, "WHY SHOULD YOU?"

G od's ways are not our ways (Proverbs 14:12; Isaiah 55:8). This is why we are told to "Trust in the LORD with ALL of our hearts and lean not on our own understanding" (what our humanity sees and hears), but "in ALL of our ways acknowledge Him and He shall direct our paths" (Proverbs 3:5–6). God reiterates this truth in different ways. For example, God says, "Sing and make music in your heart to the Lord, always giving thanks to God the Father for everything, in the name of our Lord Jesus Christ" (Ephesians 5:19b–20). In still another place God commands us to "Rejoice evermore. ... In everything give thanks: for this is the will of God in Christ Jesus concerning you (1 Thessalonians 5:16–18).

On the surface this looks completely "crazy." How can I give thanks for being molested as a child? How can I give thanks for parents who abandon children? How can I give thanks for sickness and disease? For a sibling who has taken her life? For a son or daughter on heroin? For children born with physical and emotional handicaps? For my father who divorced my mother when I was eleven? How can I give thanks for corrupt and perverted men of the cloth? For government officials who retire in opulence on the common man's money?

These are things that make absolutely no sense and defy understanding if God is a God of love. Oh, we can find answers! We live in a sin cursed world; God has made every person a free moral agent; there is a real Devil that appeals to the "me" in each of us, and the "me" is pretty self-centered and ugly. Yes, there is a Dr Jekyll and Mr. Hyde in all of us. When we yield to the "Hyde" bad things happen.

We know that these things are not of God because James tells us, "Every good and perfect gift is from above, coming down from the Father of the heavenly lights, who does not change like shifting shadows" (James 1:17).

Now what we may consider good and perfect God may not. Certainly, King Nebuchadezzar would not have considered seven years of insanity a good and perfect gift, yet God used this affliction to bring him into a personal relationship with Jehovah (Daniel 4).

Can Christians who today possess a Bible defend the wicked antics of King Henry VIII? Certainly not. Yet, the LORD, in His sovereignty, used a wicked and immoral King to place in motion that which would accomplish His purpose, putting the Word of God into the hands of people like you and me.

The reason why we can give thanks in ALL things is because God has the final word and can be trusted. We give thanks not because of the evil in the world. Not because of the injustices in the world. Not because of sickness and disease. Not because of poverty. Not because of "whatever else" is a result of sin and death (which, by the way, Jesus conquered by His death, burial and resurrection). We give thanks because the purposes of God cannot and will not be thwarted. Simply put: *God can be trusted*.

Furthermore, what God doesn't *appear* to reconcile on Earth, He has an eternity to right. Our temporal bodies and finite minds never seem to grasp the reality of a life forever in the hereafter in which God rules and reigns, with His saints, in absolute sovereignty and righteousness (Psalms 9:7; Psalms 47:8–9; Daniel 7:26–27; Revelation 19:6).

IN HIS TWENTIES, AT THE TOP OF HIS GAME AND IN LOVE, OR SO HE THOUGHT

He thought he had arrived. In his twenties and a member of one of the fastest rising rock bands the East Coast had to offer, this young man had the world by the tail. After recording their debut album and playing venues packed with adoring fans, Mr. D thought life just couldn't be any sweeter.

People loved him, or so he thought. The truth is that he had no idea what love was, but he was soon to find out. The band's business manager had become a close friend and someone Mr. D looked up to. Mr. Manager had it all — money and an unusually close and happy family.

As Mr. D's luck would have it, Mr. Manager's family included a daughter who had been dating the same guy for five years and, according to Mr. Manager, was extremely unhappy. At the time, Mr. D's success had landed him in a dating relationship with the reigning Miss New Jersey. However, when Mr. D was told that Mr. Manager's daughter was "smitten" and wanted to date him, he leaped at the opportunity. The prospect of being part of a big, happy and well-fed family was irresistible. He longed to feel the love of a family.

Mr. D lived the life of a professional musician surrounded with the faux love of strangers who loved what he did, but not necessarily who he was. Within the space of a few years, Mr. Manager had grown into a father figure for Mr. D, who never seemed to make his own father proud. (Sound familiar?) Mr. D was determined not to fail. And if opportunity looked his way, he wanted in. As fate would have it, that's exactly what happened. Mr. D and Mr. Manager's daughter soon said, "I do."

Both very young, neither Mr. D nor Mr. Manager's daughter knew how to be a husband or wife. Mr. Manager's daughter needed a Dad, one she never had. Mr. D tried to be what he could not; it was a recipe for failure. To make an increasingly bad situation worse, Mrs. D's brothers became CEOs of major companies while Mr. D's career as a rock star was quickly fading like a passing shadow. Mrs. D was continually badgering her young husband to be like this guy or that guy, basically someone he wasn't. No matter what Mr. D did, it fell short and was never good enough. Add to that the need for pick-me-ups and let-me-downs, all too familiar to the world of rock and roll, and Mr. D's drug and alcohol use increased substantially.

Raised with a Christian upbringing, an exhausted Mr. D surrendered his heart and life to Christ. Then things got really interesting. Mrs. D got more controlling while her father began to mock Mr. D.'s faith. The marriage had become a mental and psychological slugfest with Mr. Manager's family stuck in the middle. Mr. D coped with the stress by going deeper into drug and alcohol abuse. He wanted to die and on one occasion almost succeeded. It was then that Mrs. D threw her husband out of their home into the insatiable arms of addiction.

Mr. D says, "I had entered into the abyss; I was in the blackest place I had ever known. The enemy had fired his best shot and at that time I was completely defeated. On the doorstep of death, I entered into a rehabilitation facility, which at the time was fine with me. My prayer was to be taken out of this world."

Mr. D said, "While in rehab my Christian counselors explained to me that if I did not get out of this relationship (marriage) I would be dead. They were almost apologetic in their advice for they, like me, were against divorce. The inevitable happened — I was served with the divorce papers while still in rehab. Is there not a verse in the Bible that says, 'God knows what we need of before we ask'?"

It was at this dark time and place that Mr. D says, "I met the woman that I was created for." He swore he was finally home. From the very moment he saw her, his life was pulled into focus. "She was and is everything that I was made for," Mr. D says. "The Lord had made her just for me, and I for her. Our entire relationship is planted in the very soil of love. A love so beautiful it defies description. A love I had only dreamed of but had never known."

"This woman — my bride, my wife, my lover, desires me for who I am. She loves me for the person that I tried to hide from most of my life. My love for her is the purest thing I have ever known. She is my treasure from the very throne of God. She is my blessing far exceeding any measure. This is a love firmly centered in the person of Christ and I can't put it in words. I just know it is absolutely marvelous."

Yes, there are times when divorce is right.

MAXIMS LEARNED OVER
THIRTY-SEVEN YEARS OF MINISTRY

I have been in the pastorate for thirty-seven years — six as a Youth Pastor and thirty-one as a Senior Pastor. To some who have been in ministry for fifty to sixty years, I'm just a toddler — maybe a teenager. And I confess, the longer I am in the ministry the more I realize I don't know. I am forever a student. With that said, if I have learned anything in my years of living for the LORD and serving others it's this:

- God's judgments are directly relational to our pride — He hates pride.

- No man/woman is bigger than obedience to God's word.

- God's ultimate purposes will not be thwarted.

- The extent of God's discipline, be it public or private, is directly relational to our repentance.

- God will never refuse a person mercy when his/her appeal is about God's reputation and not theirs. (I am presently teaching from the Book of Revelation in our weekend worship services. This week's sermon looks at "The Four Horsemen and The Seven Seals." The third horse (black) and rider go forth with a scale in hand, judging the earth for its inequities. Now here's what's mind blowing, in the midst of God's wrath He offers mercy. God tells the horseman that he cannot hurt the oil and wine – symbolic of God's "saving grace" (Revelation 6:6). Remember the Good Samaritan, he poured oil and wine into the wounds of the man beaten and left for dead. It's a picture of God's unending love.)

- When we worry we are assuming that which belongs to God.

- There are some things that we'll never understand this side of Heaven.

- Trusting God is accepting that which we do not understand this side of Heaven.

- When we walk in "the fear of the LORD" we spare ourselves more pain and heartache than we could ever imagine.

- Vengeance is the LORD's; as long as it's in our possession it's not in His. Let it go! He'll do a better job than us anyway.

- Bitterness ends up in no one's stomach but the one who is chewing it.

- God's timing usually isn't ours, but what it is, is ALWAYS right.

- If we'll trust God with the injustices that life brings our way, whatever they may be, and leave the justice to His timing, in EVERY way we become the beneficiary.

And finally,

- What we think we'll ask God in Heaven — we won't. Because in Heaven we will know even as we are known. Look at it!

"Now we see things imperfectly, like puzzling reflections in a mirror, but then we will see everything with perfect clarity. All that I know now is partial and incomplete, but then I will know everything completely, just as God now knows me completely (1 Corinthians 12:12)." How cool is that!

I have never found this truth to fail. Whether it is a failed marriage, stolen possession, slanderous word, unspeakable abuse, and the list goes on, when we genuinely give over to God the "wrong" done to us, entrusting it to Him, He ALWAYS rights it with the least amount of ripples and damage. It is absolutely amazing. The omniscient, omnipotent, omnipresent Great Physician never ceases to heal.

In contrast, when and where we usurp God's role of judge and jury, not only do we become unattractive to those around us, but the damage is often insurmountable and irreparable.

Trusting God is believing …

"You intended to harm me, but God intended it all for good. And we know that all things work together for good to those who love God, to those who are the called according to His purpose" (Genesis 50:20a; Romans 8:28).

Today Mr. D. and his wife are facing new challenges brought on by the aftermath of failed marriages. But as I watch their desire to please God, and trust Him no matter what those challenges may bring, there is this deep seated peace that says, "All will be well," for the best of all is that God is with them (Psalms 46:7; 46:11).

Yes, God's will, God's way, to His glory is always the best way. Trust Him. He cannot fail.

Questions

1) In the opening story of this chapter, Mr. D was disillusioned by the glitz of stardom; eventually it ate him up. Why is it so difficult for people whose careers are of celebrity status to keep their marriages? What can a person do, whose life is focused on them (celebrity status), do to safeguard their marriage?

2) Mr. D thought he was in love. What killed love for Mr. D? What attracted Mr. D to the woman to whom he is now married?

3) The author of this book, *WDIR*, shares a number of truths (fourteen), which he has learned from his years in ministry. Which of the fourteen relates to your life, and why?

4) What will be the 'one' question you will ask God when you get to Heaven? Why does the author say, "What we think we'll ask God in Heaven — we won't?"

5) After reading this chapter, what question would you ask?

CHAPTER FIFTEEN

୧ଓ

REMAINING IN MINISTRY AFTER DIVORCE

A SECOND CHANCE IN MORE WAYS THAN ONE

I was only twenty-six years old. My lovely bride of five months was nineteen. I was the new youth director for Mt Pleasant Church, just outside of Atlantic City, NJ.

Nearly seven years later God called Sheryl and me to return to my hometown and start a church. With two very small children (Joel, two and Noelle, seven months), many thought we misheard God. With no promise of an income or place to live, it made absolutely no sense to well-meaning people to uproot — especially at this time in our young family's life.

I remember when our mentor, Dr. Eugene D. Huber, spoke at GCCC's one-year anniversary. With tears in his eyes he said to our young and exuberant congregation of one-hundred people, "Now I understand why God called your pastor to start this church."

Well, time to quit reminiscing and get to the story. In our first year at Mt. Pleasant a young man came through our youth group whom I had the privilege of getting to know at a distance, and marrying. Oops, let me correct that statement before my wife does. I didn't marry him or his bride, I officiated their wedding.

When we moved from Pleasantville to Pitman (one hour's drive from Pleasantville), Mr. M came to Sheryl and me and said that he felt God wanted him to join us in starting the new church, and that he would help wherever needed. And what a tremendous help he was. Our first paid employee, Mr. M made a whopping $10 a week to cover the cost of gas from Pleasantville to Pitman. Mr. M wore many hats: church secretary, treasurer, and youth director, all of which he did very well. His wife directed our nursery and helped clean the church.

However, there were childhood issues, unbeknown to me, that would manifest themselves from time to time, most notably as anger. I don't recall the exact situation at the end, just that it was pretty ugly. The final result was Mr. M turning in his keys.

From that time forward, the downward spiral hit full speed. You know what they say, "It's not the fall, but the landing that does you in!" And land he did! Two kids and nine years later, Mr. M found himself separated from his wife and children and addicted to "little white pills." Sometimes he would drown his pain with fifty to seventy Percocet at a time. Wanting to die

— but not wanting to die. He really wanted to live, but at this point didn't know how.

The years of childhood abuse, which included incest, finally surfaced in behaviors unacceptable to God and the Church. The price was heavy. Mr. M lost his marriage, his job at the church, and most of his close personal and professional relationships. However, in the midst of his prodigal behaviors, God kept a few friends close by and never let go of him. The day came when Mr. M decided to do something about the pain of his past and the promise of a future.

Today Mr. M is happily remarried, has a marvelous relationship with his children, and for over a decade was fully employed by our Church overseeing the finances! Who would give the responsibility of finances to an addict? Oh yeah, he also ran our Recovery Ministry.

Now is Mr. M fully "normalized?" No! But if the truth were known, all of us have some type of spiritual and emotional abnormality that needs Holy Ghost fixing. Only God is perfect. Sorry, but they're the facts. I often think, "Look how you've given Mr. M another chance. Look at how far he's come. Who would have ever dreamed?" Thank God for second, third, fourth ... seven, no, seven x seven chances.

I am humbled over and over again at God's pursuing, persevering, and perfecting love. It just never lets go. Indeed what He began in us He completes (Philippians 1:6). And if He doesn't get it done on this side of the Jordan, He will when we cross over. The problem doesn't lie with God but our stubbornness, our selfish pride and rebellion. Well, I'd better quit preaching — I'm too often the choir.

The promise of Romans 11:29 remains true, "…the gifts and calling of God are irrevocable."

As the hymn writer put it:

I stand amazed in the presence Of Jesus the Nazarene,
And wonder how He could love me,
A sinner, condemned, unclean.
O how marvelous! O how wonderful!
And my song shall ever be:
O how marvelous! O how wonderful!
Is my Savior's love for me!

Yes, our God is not just the God of second chances; He's the God of many chances in more ways than we could ever deem imaginable. Yes, there is a place for the divorced in ministry. I could name many well-known ministers who pastor large, some mega, churches. If I were to give their names here you would recognize them. Today they continue in local church ministry used by God to accomplish His purposes.

Now, here's the reality — they are probably better ministers because of their divorce than they were before. Divorce is a very humbling, sometimes humiliating, experience. I'm reminded of these words spoken by our Savior: "I tell you, this sinner, not the Pharisee, returned home justified before God. For those who exalt themselves will be humbled, and those who humble themselves will be exalted" (Luke 18:14).

AN EXTREMELY CONTROVERSIAL SUBJECT

When the Apostle Paul addressed controversial issues in the church, he said on one occasion, "I, not the LORD," and on another occasion: "I have no command from the LORD, but I give my judgment as one who by God's mercy is trustworthy" (Corinthians 7:12; 7:23). In other words, I cannot say, "Thus saith the LORD," but what I can say is, "As a minister of the Gospel I believe I understand the mind and heart of God on this matter."

Certainly I am not the Apostle Paul, nor would I be so foolishly arrogant as to put myself in the same sentence other than I am a blood washed, blood bought "holy one" (saint); not because I have earned it or am worthy of it, but because it is God's free gift to all who believe. And I am a believer.

With that said, I will not put this in stone, but I believe that what I have to say has come through the crucible of decades of studying God's Word (all of it), observing God's ways in matters pertaining to divorce — He always has the last word bringing truth into the light, and a genuine search for the heart of God where divorce has touched the lives of those in full-time ministry and leadership positions within the Church.

SHOULD A PERSON IN MINISTRY GOING THROUGH A DIVORCE BE BROUGHT UNDER CHURCH DISCIPLINE?

This question is posed to me more often than I'd like, which tells us something about the state of the modern church.

However, it is a question that needs to be answered. Many believe that a person who is going through a divorce while in ministry should be brought under "church discipline" or "removed" from their place of service.

Recently, the former quarterback of the Atlanta Falcons was in a similar position because of his involvement in dog fighting. Some felt that he was welcome to return to society but not as a player in the NFL; he had disqualified himself from professional football, forever. Some would hold to that position within the church pertaining to those having gone through a divorce — a divorced person can return to society and live a normal life, but he/she cannot return to ministry; it is off limits. The real issue here is finding God's position, which is His heart.

So, where do we begin? First, there is no hard and fast rule in these situations because we are given no specific examples. Therefore, I believe each case must be weighed individually and handled with sensitivity and care. In looking for God's heart we do have situational examples: Samson, Judah (son of Jacob), King David, Abner (Captain of King Saul's army), Herod (King of Judea), the woman at the well, the woman caught in adultery, and the man of Corinth who was committing fornication with his mother (most likely his stepmother).

Second, because God hates divorce, we have established the following truths for obvious reasons:

- God is love and divorce means love and trust have been fractured.

- Crush love and you crush the heart of God.

- No matter how smooth or justified a divorce may be, those who know, or are a part of the family, become a victim in some measure.

With these truths in mind, we must be careful not to play judge and jury when we have not walked in another's shoes (Matthew 7:1; Luke 6:37). Believe me, God will be judge and jury and have the last word; nobody gets over on God. We don't need to usurp His role. Where there is a direct violation of God's Word, then we have a responsibility before the LORD to direct the person caught up in the transgression in the way of the LORD. After that, we must let God be God.

In cases where things are not clear and there appears to be just and scriptural cause for divorce, we must love, guide, and support, seeking His will, His way so that life can be brought to the husband, wife, family, children, and all involved (Jeremiah 29:11; John 10:10).

Because we have no specific examples of men or women in the Bible in ministry positions having gone through a divorce, let's look at a few scenarios of people called by God that could very well be applicable, and while doing so lay hold of the heart of God.

LAYING HOLD OF THE HEART OF GOD

Samson: Here is a man whose lifestyle obviously grieved God. He slept with a prostitute, wed a Philistine, had an ongoing affair with Delilah, and broke his Nazarite vow in all but one place. (We have no record that he drank wine.) Yet, God does not remove his calling or him from office. He was an appointed judge until the day of his death (Judges 13-16).

Judah: Judah slept with his daughter-in-law, Tamar, whom he thought was a prostitute. Yet, God does not remove from Judah the appointment to be the father of the Messiah. And is through the tribe of Judah, not Joseph, that the Messiah comes into the world (Psalms 78:67–68).

King David: We all know the story of David and Bath-sheba — David committed adultery, murder, and took another man's wife. Yet, God did not remove his calling or his office (kingship). Scripture tells us that when Christ returns and Israel is restored that "David my servant will be king over the people" (Ezekiel 34:23-24; Ezekiel 37:24).

King Herod: Herod was a wicked man and ruthless king. John the Baptist rebuked him for having his brother's wife. Yet, God does not permit anyone to remove Herod's calling (leadership) or his position (king). Now, there is a day when God removes Herod, but it is an act of God, not man. (Mark 6:18; Acts 12:23).

Let's look at one more:

The man committing adultery with his mother: Most Bible scholars believe this was not his biological mother, but his father's wife who was not his mother. However, no one truly knows. Paul, the voice of God in this instance, tells the congregation to remove the fornicator from their fellowship until there is genuine repentance. Now, keep in mind, there is no question here as to who is sinning and the nature of the sin. The man is removed, repents, and is restored to fellowship (2 Corinthians 2:6–11).

Whether or not this man has a position of leadership in the church is debatable. However, he was obviously well known enough that he was a topic of conversation in the church.

For our purpose here, let's not get caught up in the man's sin; let's look for the heart of God. The transgressor was chastised because God's desire was to bring about repentance in the man, his mother, and the Church at large (1 Corinthians 5:1). Furthermore, Paul pleads with the Church to restore him to whatever position he held before his discipline. And in so doing, God's forgiveness would be witnessed and felt by all, as well as Satan's schemes brought to naught (2 Corinthians 2:10–11).

In all of these examples we see the heart of God — God's gifts and calling are irrevocable despite the enemy's attempts to highjack them. Repentance and restoration are God's heart. When this takes place, Satan's schemes are thwarted and God's kingdom advances. Sadly, the church often refuses to demonstrate true forgiveness; they talk about it but they don't demonstrate it. The result is that the church loses a gift from God as the repentant sinner is shunned and never allowed back into his/her calling. Because the church refuses to forgive, everyone then suffers loss. The sinner, as in this instance, however, must demonstrate genuine repentance. Too many times it's as much the transgressor's fault in not returning to his/her calling as it is the church's. A person can't be restored to the position of his/her calling UNTIL they have asked and lived true repentance.

In these matters of searching out sin, I have found this to be true: No one gets over on God. He will bring sin to light in His timing and handle it in His way. This does not mean we should turn our heads when sin is brought to our attention; we can't. Eli lost the priesthood because he refused to remove his sons when they were practicing idolatry and adultery in the House of God. With that said, when we suspect something is not right but don't have proof, if we'll wait on the LORD and let God be God, He will circumcise the sin with little or no pain. Furthermore, the body of Christ continues, strengthened rather than weakened.

IF YOU HAVEN'T WALKED IN THEIR SHOES . . .

To accuse a man or woman of sin because they are going through a divorce or have gone through a divorce when you do not know his/her heart, or pass judgment on a decision he/she has made when you do not have the facts, or have not walked in his/her shoes, is in itself sin. Again, divorce is NOT necessarily sin, however, what leads to it is!

Many will point to the vows made at the altar as a weapon for judgment; yet, it's amazing how we pick and choose the vows we can break and not break, like church membership. Ecclesiastes 5 does not differentiate between vows and neither does God (i.e. Saul and the Gibeonites). Church membership is a covenant (a marriage if you please), yet people break that vow all the time without remorse or repentance. However, it is also clear that vows are a two-way street; they are covenants. When one breaks the covenant he/she is loosed from the covenant. Some examples are God and King Saul, God and Israel, God and Solomon, the husband and wife in 1 Corinthians 7, and the list goes on.

I am not suggesting divorce for those in ministry. God hates divorce! However, some spouses are far greater victims, as well as their children, when they have biblical grounds to do so and don't. As has been said previously, God has not called his children to death, but life. The only place He has called us to die is to self so that we can be united with Him — the very picture of baptism and the very picture of walking together with Christ to fulfill His calling upon one's life.

MY RESPONSIBILITY AS A PASTOR

My responsibility to those going through divorce while in ministry is to be there as a pastor and friend. I cannot live their lives for them. I can, however, give Godly, biblical counsel and do my best to see that they continue in a right relationship with their LORD regardless of their marital status. In some instances it is wise for a person, or couple, to step down from their visible place of ministry so that those with whom they work, and the church, are not negatively affected during the divorce. This also gives the person, or couple, an opportunity to search his/her heart before God and rest in His will free from the activity of service. However, I believe that this is a decision that must be arrived at by the Senior Pastor, Advisory Board, and person(s) involved.

Sheryl and I have made it a point over the years to make ourselves available to those who are struggling in their marriages, particularly those who are in ministry, even at the expense of our own schedules. We will continue to do so, because successful marriages that last "until death does [them] part," have been a priority in God's heart since creation.

MY HEART'S PRAYER

Father in Heaven, my prayer is that the homes and relationships in our churches today would model your heart by removing the selfishness and prideful dysfunction that dismembers homes and destroys our culture. LORD, some are dealing with years of poor modeling, some have lived with hatred, including verbal, emotional, and sexual abuse. Some wonder if You even exist — what they have seen is so cruel, so nasty, so vile that they hate You almost as much as they hate those who have abused them.

They have never heard the words, "I love you." They have never heard the words, "You're beautiful!" or "You're handsome." They have never heard the words, "You can do it!"

Let them see the heart of the Cross. Open their eyes to see that whatever pain they have experienced, no matter how ugly or vile, You took that anguish upon Yourself on the Cross. Let them see that You are not unsympathetic to their hurts and that You major in making the ugly beautiful; that nothing is impossible with You. That there is nothing in the whole wide world that Your grace is not capable of swallowing up.

And LORD, where they feel unworthy, where they feel they cannot be forgiven, may they see Your blood as a detergent that knows no stain it cannot remove. May Your love be deeper than any pit in which they find themselves. May even in this moment, this time of prayer, they sense Your mercy and presence.

Father, for those who have lost their position in ministry — whatever the reason may be, grant them once again a place in Your Church. Let Your family, for whom You died, be receptive to their return and may their calling come to life in greater power than ever before. Allow the lessons learned make us better, more understanding and wiser teachers. May our repentance be genuine and lasting.

By fulfilling our callings, let us close the jaws of Hell and open the gates of Heaven. Grant us the grace and strength to do Your will, Your way, to Your glory. In Jesus' name, Amen!

QUESTIONS

1) In the opening story of this chapter Mr. M is mentioned as the first paid employee of GCCC. Why did Pastor Bruce employ him? Knowing the story, after Mr. M's past caught up with him, would you have taken the risk of hiring him again? If yes, why? If no, why? Remaining steadfast or faltering, do you believe a person who's been divorced can remain or return to ministry?

2) Do you know of someone whose life has been destroyed by an addiction who today has put away that besetting sin? If so, would you say they are now 'normal'?

3) Many in the Church feel that a person going through divorce should be brought before Church 'discipline' or even 'removed' from their position of service. The author feels that in the case of 'removal' each case must be weighted individually. Do you agree? If so, why? If not, why?

4) The author closes this chapter with a prayer. What part of the prayer can you relate to? Why?

5) After reading this chapter, what question would you ask?

CHAPTER SIXTEEN

❧

THE FIVE-FOLD PURPOSE

I remember making light of it, "So, you're the woman at the well?" Well, it wasn't funny to her. But the truth is she had been married four times. Was this Hollywood or Church? We could enumerate the reasons why this attractive and "with it" blond failed at four attempts at marriage, but that is not the point of this illustration.

Today, this "woman at the well" is happily married and serves faithfully in our church and her community, as does her husband. She is not proud that she is now married for the fifth time and certainly doesn't shout it from the rooftops, but she doesn't hide in her bedroom either. So resting in the fact that God has a blueprint already designed just for her, and her husband, they are determined to not allow the enemy to steal from them what is rightfully theirs in Christ. Faithful to one another, faithful to the church, and faithful to serving, this couple continues to pursue God's calling upon their lives. And mercifully, our gracious LORD is using them for His glory and the advancement of His kingdom.

Whenever I think of Mr. and Mrs. S, I'm reminded that for those who understand God's heart on divorce, walk humbly in His forgiveness, and seek to break the generational pattern — life springs forth out of death. Do you recall the aftermath of Lazarus' resurrection from the grave? Many were brought to belief in "the Way."

So, when couples who break the pattern of divorce by loving "unto death does [them] part," or who hand down a legacy of no divorce, exemplify a happy and loving home, the world not only becomes a better place and its children better adapted, but it becomes a God-like place where the oneness that the Father, Son, and Holy Spirit have in Heaven, is enjoyed down here on Earth.

Truly, to do the will of the Father benefits everyone, not just the obedient disciple. The beauty of the Christian message is, no matter how many times we've blown it, "… all things work for the good of those who love God and have been called according to His purpose" (Romans 8:28). Now with that said, there still remains the law of "sowing and reaping" (Galatians 6:7). Let me explain so that no one is disillusioned by or misconstrues that promise. Here's what I mean: King David committed adultery with another man's wife, and then killed the man. These actions are not free from consequences — there were ramifications. In fact, many, of which we will not take the time to elaborate on. It's the law of sowing and reaping: "Whatsoever a man sows that shall he reap" (Galatians 6:7). By the way, women are included in that maxim, too. (I know — my humor is really bad.)

Back to Mrs. S who is married to husband number five. Here are the facts, if you were to sit down with Mrs. S and have an honest and in-depth conversation, you would hear the woes — the reaping. That's the irreversible biblical truth/law set forth at Creation (Genesis 1:11-12). Yet, here is still another law/truth — God's mercies, which are new every morning (Lamentations 3:22-23), can take the reaping and bring forth a miraculous harvest.

Let's go back to King David and his adulterous affair with Bathsheba, wife of the mighty warrior, Uriah. There are only five women named in the genealogy of Jesus the Christ, and one of them is Bathsheba. David had ten wives. From whom does the Messiah come? Bathsheba. Yes, God's ways are not ours. As they say in Montana, "You betcha!" We know not why God chose to bring the Messiah from Bathsheba and not one of David's other wives. We could speculate but that may suggest unfounded truths about his other nine wives unfairly. However, as we see the story of Solomon succeeding David, we see a very humble and wise woman in Bathsheba.

What we can rightly conjecture is that she had given her sin to the Heavenly Father, sought His forgiveness, asking for divine intervention and got it. I can only imagine her prayer life. Yes, the reaping was in keeping with the transgression for both David and Bathsheba, but so was the reaping of repentance. (I like that phrase – "the reaping of repentance." Sounds like another book to me.) God honored the latter working out all things for this king and queen's good. And, He'll do the same for you.

Back to the reassuring truth that *today* we can walk in obedience to God's Word as set from in the Bible and live out His plan for our lives regardless of our yesterdays. When we do so, it's absolutely amazing how God will put peace in the midst of turmoil, make pluses out of minuses, and create the miraculous out of, yes, even our everyday messes. Wow! What a gracious and merciful God. There is none like Him. He is great and greatly to be praised!

The purpose of this book has been five-fold:

1. To understand God's heart on divorce (Genesis 2:24; Malachi 2:16);

2. To remove the guilt placed on those who have suffered the pain of divorce, which is not in keeping with the truth set down in Holy Scriptures (Deuteronomy 32:19; Nehemiah 8:3; 2 Timothy 2:15);

3. To break the chain of cyclical sin and dysfunction (iniquity and infirmity) passed on from generation to generation as a result of divorce (Exodus 20:5; Nehemiah 9:2; Isaiah 50:1; Isaiah 53:4; Romans 6:19);

4. To bring life to those living in death. Truth begets truth; the lie begets the lie. Jesus came into the world not to condemn it but to save it (2 Chronicles 36:4; Ezra 10; Nehemiah 7:64; Jude 1:23; Luke 6:45; Matthew 5:37; James 3:11–12; John 3:17);

5. To bring God pleasure (worship) with our lives regardless of the disasters that life, or we, may have met or meet. (Psalms 38:4; Psalms 51:13; Genesis 50:20; Romans 8:28; Hebrews 11:21).

I love the words of the "man after God's own heart." You (God) forgave the guilt of my sin (Psalms 32:5). What is "the guilt of my sin?" The inability to forgive oneself. God granted David the grace to forgive himself. In Psalms 51:13 David, after resting in God's forgiveness, says, "Then I will teach transgressors Your ways."

Truly, every blessing God gives to us He gives so that we may pass it on. Someone wisely said, "When you fail to invest what God gives you, God loses His return and you lose the rewards you would have enjoyed" (Matthew 25:15). Everything God gives you — including forgiveness, a new beginning, and a future of hope and blessings, is meant to be multiplied.

It is my prayer that in reading this book you have found answers to the questions that have haunted you, allowed God to remove the self-condemnation that we so often inflict upon ourselves, and, in so doing, once again walk in the liberating freedom of God's love and forgiveness ... and then pass it on. Remember, God finds a plus in every pile of minuses. If He can, so can we! For His power works in us to do His will, His way, for His glory (2 Timothy 1:9, Ephesians 2:10).

QUESTIONS

1) In the opening story of this chapter, the reader is introduced to a woman who had been married four times. Think of those whom you know who have been divorced, which person has been married the most number of times? Would you be so bold as to state 'why'? Was it him/her or just a string of bad choices?

2) If you've been divorced, would you say the reason for your divorce was you or your spouse? If neither, then what was it?

3) If you've been divorced, what did you learn from your first marriage you're determined not to repeat in your present, or if it is apropos, next marriage?

4) What is the "five-fold" purpose of this book, *When Divorce is Right?*

5) After reading this chapter, what question would you ask?

CHAPTER SEVENTEEN

ACKNOWLEDGEMENTS

To be totally honest, I know that we are to be "anxious for nothing," but if there is any part of this book that makes me anxious — it is this: the acknowledgements. Where does one begin? How do you acknowledge all who contribute to what others consider an accomplishment? Surely someone will get left out! So, if you've contributed to this project and have gone unnamed, forgive me, it certainly was not intentional.

Where do I begin? I am going to leave the most important person till last — does not the Good Book say, "the first shall be last and the last shall be first?" Indeed, in this case that is true.

I must first start with my family. I had a grandmother, Anna E. Smith, who, according to the Church was a *saint* — yes, she met every qualification. Now, to God every blood washed, blood bought, born-again believer is a saint. I remember as a child spending time at her home. She would be on her knees praying. I would say, "Grand Mom, aren't you done yet?" My mother, who was a college English major, had not yet corrected my sentence structure. It is that heritage which implanted in me the truth of God's Word and the power of prayer at a very early age.

Add to that a godly mother, Mary, and father, John, who saw that we were in Church nearly every time the doors were open, coupled with a life that paralleled what they taught – and you understand why I must acknowledge my heritage. I saw my mother and father read their Bibles and pray every day. It was an honor so many never have. Still others may see parents attend church, read their Bibles and pray, but the lifestyle of the parent doesn't parallel what is preached. That was not so in my home. My father and mother lived their religion. They lived their faith without hypocrisy. It was and is a gift from above (I pray my children say the same about me).

At the time of this book project (2009), my father, age eighty-seven, went to his real home for Christmas. He lived a full and rewarding life influencing thousands with a quiet and gentle spirit. He was a true Nathaniel (John 1:47). While taking time to review this final manuscript, my mother passed one month shy of her 94th birthday. She was an amazing person. Up to ten days before "going home," she was answering our Church's Prayer Hot Line and sending cards to the sick and shut-in. Speaking of my mother, I would be remiss if I didn't tell this story. When I put it in our GCCC News (Bulletin), I entitled it *There Is Something In The Numbers:*

Acknowledgements

My father took the Glory Train to Heaven at 4:20 am. Mom passed into Glory at 4:20 am.

Mom's room number while on "support" in the Hospital was 420, and when they moved her to "comfort care," her room number was 402 (same floor). Now add to that Mom was born in 4/1920 and Easter this year was 4/20 and ... well, should I really say this on a Church bulletin page? Play the lottery! Just make sure you tithe on your win.

To my sister and brother-in-law, Sandy and Jerry Clendenen, who have faithfully stood by my side in support of my calling through thick and thin; my father and mother-in-law, Stephen and Anita Farnelli (who have also passed into Glory), to the pastors in my teen years — Reverend Earl Watts and Dr. George Riddell, to my mentors in ministry —— Dr. Gene Huber and his wife Susan (God's chosen instructors), to an Advisory Board, Pastoral Staff and congregation who have believed and supported me through the years — I acknowledge their huge contribution to my life and this project.

How do I adequately express what it means when people tell me, "Pastor, you can't believe how you changed my life!" I have simply learned to say, "Thank you, but let's give credit where credit is due — it's Jesus who has changed your life; I am only the messenger." Then there are those who say, "I can't wait to read your book! Make sure I get the first signed copy." These words make all the heartaches of ministry worthywhile – and there are many. Hey, at least I knew at that moment there was one copy sold. (Over ½ million books are published every year in the USA, less than 2% sell more than 500 books.)

Next to God, I am eternally grateful for my wife, Sheryl, who has sacrificially given of herself to see that my calling to ministry remains unimpeded. When the Scriptures say, "He who finds a wife finds a good thing," I understand that truth and blessing. When we married, my wife was a nineteen-year-old phlegmatic, and the most beautiful creature on God's green planet earth. Her strength, character, and faith are deeply settled. She is the best Christian I know — well, most of the time. She'll use those words against me if I don't qualify that statement. Only kidding! She has forgiven me, and others, for things most women would have crucified their husbands for. She is a wonderful mother and the best office manager I know. She loves the LORD, and me, in a deeper and greater measure every day — it blows me away. I would not be where I am today, as a minister or personally, without my wife. She truly is my helpmate and gift from Above. Every day that is added to my life, I thank God in greater measure for the blessing I, and so many others, have in my wife, Sheryl.

I would be remiss if I did not mention my children, Joel and Noelle. My children, like their mother, have sacrificed immeasurably. They have understood the demands of ministry and have never resented it. Today they faithfully serve at the church (Joel is the Executive Administrator), and are a constant source of support and encouragement. I am pretty sure Joel will take over the pulpit when I've stepped down from its weekly duties, but that will be his decision not mine. (Not because he is my son, but he is one of the finest preachers I have ever heard.) Noelle is every parent's dream — adventurous, effervescent, and beautiful. I'm not sure where God's calling will direct her, but wherever it is she'll bless many.

Now, upon reading this book, I may be in deep trouble since both of their stories open chapters. But here again, our children's lives reveal the unchanging truth of Romans 8:28, and is seen in full living color, HD and 3-D modes. Yes, God has used their trials to keep Sheryl and me humble, less judgmental, and more like Him. Joel and Noelle, we love you deeply.

Then there are those who have made this project possible by giving countless hours with little or no remuneration: Rick Kern, a brilliant man with a gifted pen, whose path I crossed at a Faith & Action (Washington, DC). In just a few minutes our hearts were united in purpose as we spoke of the things of God and the contemporary life issues that face our culture today, which desperately need God's perspective. It was Rick saying, "I'm a writer, send me your stuff and I'll see what I can do," that served as the catalyst to write this book and the *Hijacked Life – Rescue Your Dream* series.

Meditations in All that He Is was well on its way with the help of Lisa Moore when I had met Mr. Kern. Rick has been a second set of eyes, a fresh pen when thoughts didn't quite make sense, and an agent of sorts as we have followed the LORD in seeking a publisher.

Thanks Rick! Words fail to express what you and your contribution have meant to me through all of this. (All of which required much patience — there have been far too many interruptions along the way.)

There would be no *Hijacked Life – Rescue Your Dream* series without Jason Hannath — who found me when Rick and I were looking for a publisher (that's a story in itself); Jason's vision is far bigger than mine — I just want to write and bring healing to confused and shattered lives, he wants to rescue the dream of every person on the planet whose life has been 'hijacked' by the tragedies and transgressions of life. I love Jason's zeal. Let's add to that team Roger Chasteen, a friend of Jason's who, after reading these book projects, believed that they were worthy of publication.

Last but not least in this publishing world is "cwebster." (I'm not sure if cwebster is a man or woman, but my guess is CW is the latter — there's just something about the comments.)

Whatever, CW's insights and edits were nothing short of superb. Great job cwebster! Thanks!

Oh, how can I forget? Warm words of appreciation are in order to Cheryl McFall who proofs my sermon every week, looking for grammatical errors and things that may make sense to me but no one else – she has been an excellent teacher, Jim Atkinson, Diane Deshler, Michele Galasso (who approached this book as one who was <u>un</u>familiar with Church jargon), and Dr Gordon and Sue Henry (whose knowledge of the Scriptures brought a level of accuracy needed for a project of this nature). After all was said and done — surely we caught all of the errors, right? Wrong! To our embarrassment, Sharon

Acknowledgements

Hervold found far more grammatical and wording errors than any of us wanted to attest to. (And I suspect some of you reading *When Divorce is Right* will find other *mistakes* when reading this book. Hey, if you do, write the Publisher not me.) Back to the GCCC Review Team — you guys are wonderful!

Also, a special thanks to Woody and Evelyn Vanaman and Guy and Jill Leone who opened their summer homes to me so that I could work free from the distractions that come from working at home or the office. You guys are a blessing!

Lastly, but most importantly, I acknowledge my LORD and Savior Jesus Christ. But for His grace, I confess to you, my life would be shipwrecked. The "me" in me would have sunken this ship a long time ago. His persistent, pursuing, and persevering love has followed me from the time I said "yes" to Him at not-quite-five-years-of-age until now, some sixty years later. There are times He could have easily put me to shame, but instead He covered my sin and shame. When in my stubbornness I insisted on doing it my way, He patiently bore with me — guiding and hearing the repentant cry of my heart. How can we understand or know the measure of His love? We cannot.

Each man should believe that His calling is the greatest in the world — and to him/her it should be. In fact, we ALL have the same calling: "Follow me" Jesus said, "and I will make you fishers of men" (Matthew 4:19). With that said, we must understand that although we each have the 'same calling', we each have 'different pulpits' in which to fulfill that calling. To me, God has granted me the highest calling any man could ask for — teacher-pastor. Many times as a pastor our words are like God's to the listening ear. We are often looked at like a god, no matter how often we speak of our frailties. Yet, out of this profession (calling) the LORD changes lives — forever. It is absolutely mind-boggling and miraculous.

It is from the crucible of this Pastor's life, the observations made, the lessons learned, all within the context of God's infallible Word, that I acknowledge His part in this writing project.

If I may, let me close with these words to my Lord:

"Jesus, You are my best friend, I am eternally indebted to You. I only wish that my flesh was not so weak and that I could say, "I have never failed You," but I can't. What I can say is, "Thank You for never failing me. Thank you for never leaving or forsaking me. Thank You for a love that I will never comprehend this side of Heaven. Thank You for taking my screw-ups and making something good out of them. Thank You for hearing me when I pray. Thank You for the promise, "the best of all is You are with us." Thank You for the promise of life after death — how empty life would be if this was the end. Thank You for the words I cannot find right now, but I so deeply feel. Thank You for being my very best friend. I love You."

QUESTIONS

1) In this chapter the author speaks of his godly legacy. Do you have a legacy? Is it godly? If it is not, what are you doing to change it?

2) The author makes a 'light moment' out of playing the lottery using the numbers 4-2-0. On a more serious note, has there ever been a time when the numbers, or whatever, aligned in such a way that you knew something was divine about it all? What was that moment and what made it divine?

3) Is there any one statement of verse that changed your life for the better? Is there any one person whose influence has changed your life for the better? Is there any one person who has impacted your life for the worse? How did you overcome that 'negative' and 'damaging' seed?

4) The author closes this chapter and book by saying, "Jesus, You are my best friend, [and] I am eternally indebted to You." Have you found Jesus to be your best friend? Why?

5) After reading this chapter, what question would you ask?